PRAISE FOR *F**K IT* AND JOHN C. PARKIN

'Everyone can relate to F**k It.'
THE TIMES – SATURDAY REVIEW

'This book makes me smile and, more importantly, clicks my brain into positive mode.'
FEARNE COTTON

'The self-help phenomenon we can all swear by.'
EVENING STANDARD

'"F**k It". I was practising the words. They rolled around my head. We need to say "F**k It" when we're out of sync with the natural world; it helps us go with the flow.'
THE OBSERVER

'John combines Wayne Hemingway's style with Eddie Izzard's flights of surrealism.'
THE GUARDIAN

'Self-help for the time-poor and psycho-babble intolerant.'
MARIE CLAIRE

'Something making you unhappy? One man's F**k It therapy teaches us to let go.'
METRO

Revised and updated edition

F**K IT

ALSO BY JOHN C. PARKIN

BOOKS

F**k It: Be at Peace with Life, Just as It Is (2018)

F**k It: Do What You Love (2016)

F**k It Is the Answer (2014)

F**k It Therapy (2012)

The Way of F**k It (2009)

AUDIOBOOKS

F**k It Therapy (2015)

The F**k It Show (2010)

Revised and updated edition

F**K IT

THE ULTIMATE SPIRITUAL WAY

John C. Parkin

HAY HOUSE

Carlsbad, California • New York City
London • Sydney • New Delhi

Published in the United Kingdom by:
Hay House UK Ltd, The Sixth Floor, Watson House,
54 Baker Street, London W1U 7BU
Tel: +44 (0)20 3927 7290; Fax: +44 (0)20 3927 7291; www.hayhouse.co.uk

Published in the United States of America by:
Hay House Inc., PO Box 5100, Carlsbad, CA 92018-5100
Tel: (1) 760 431 7695 or (800) 654 5126
Fax: (1) 760 431 6948 or (800) 650 5115; www.hayhouse.com

Published in Australia by:
Hay House Australia Pty Ltd, 18/36 Ralph St, Alexandria NSW 2015
Tel: (61) 2 9669 4299; Fax: (61) 2 9669 4144; www.hayhouse.com.au

Published in India by:
Hay House Publishers India, Muskaan Complex,
Plot No.3, B-2, Vasant Kunj, New Delhi 110 070
Tel: (91) 11 4176 1620; Fax: (91) 11 4176 1630; www.hayhouse.co.in

A catalogue record for this book is available from the British Library.

Tradepaper ISBN: 978-1-78817-714-6
E-book ISBN: 978-1-78817-720-7
Audiobook ISBN: 978-1-78817-715-3

Interior illustrations: 214–226 © Gaia Pollini; 232–233 © Michelangelo
Gratton/Getty Images; 234–235 © Shutterstock

Dedicated to Gaia, Leone and Arco

CONTENTS

Contents

THE BEGINNING

Your Beginning: Say F**k It to Something Now

When you say F**k It, you let go of your hold on something – usually something that's causing you pain.

When you say F**k It, you give in to the flow of life – you stop doing what you don't want to do, you finally do what you've always wanted to do, and you stop listening to people and listen to yourself.

When you say F**k It, you carry out a spiritual act (the ultimate one, actually) because you give up, let go, stop resisting and relax back into the natural flow of life itself (otherwise known as the Tao, Spirit, etc.).

When you say F**k It, you stop worrying (generally), give up wanting (mainly) and end up being darn happy to be yourself in the present moment (if you're lucky).

So, before we jump, arm in arm, into this swimming pool of F**k It wisdom, have a go yourself now. Say F**k It to something. It could be something small (take a trip to the fridge and gobble down that cheesecake) or big (take a trip to that lazy pig you call your partner and tell them to take a walk).

Say F**k It to something… anything. And feel the freedom and release that it brings. Multiply that to the power of 10 – imagine feeling like that for most of the time – and you have an idea of what you're getting into.

SAY F**K IT TO SOMETHING NOW.

And, last thing before we jump then, let's SHOUT together: Fuuuuccccckkkkkkkk liiittttttttttttttttt!

My Beginning: the Epiphany of Seeing F**k It as a Spiritual Way

What you've just read would have been some of the first words I wrote for the first draft of the first edition of this book. I wrote those first words in late 2004, then wrote more over the next couple of years, and the first edition was published in 2008.

You'll read many of the original words from back then in this book. But with other words I've written since, too, including many chapters I'm writing for this edition, in the summer of 2021.

When I wrote those original words, our twin boys were young, and there's a reference in the text to Leone speaking his first English sentences to me (as I was tapping away, writing the first edition of this book). And now our boys are at university in England. And by the time you read this, maybe they'll be writing books, shooting movies and singing songs of their own out there in the world.

This book continues to be read around the world (29 countries and counting) because the message at the heart of it is timeless, and timelessly exciting.

I wrote the book back then in order to capture the excitement of this 'epiphany': that saying the profanity F**k It is spiritual. I wanted to capture this excitement and wisdom for myself as much as for anyone else. I could sense that what I was experiencing was fresh and powerful. So I wrote it down. And then many others found it fresh and exciting, and they told others about it, and here we are.

And such powerful observed truths can last.

The poems of Rumi feel fresh today (I can't say 'as fresh' because I have no idea how they were received nearly 800 years ago).

People are still living by the truths of ancient religious texts, and there are timeless truths in there.

Sadly sometimes views that are outdated and bigoted can also last. If only God had been asked by His publisher to come in and do a revised edition of the Bible every few years, you might not have people in the 21st century thinking that being gay is wrong, or that wives should obey their husbands, or whatever other archaic, outrageous and hurtful nonsense sits alongside some fair-to-middling self-help advice (I remember and rather liked 'Do not worry about tomorrow, for tomorrow will worry about itself. Each day has enough trouble of its own.' Matthew 6:34).

Not that I'm comparing myself to Rumi, or even God, but, for the time I'm on this planet, you've got me coming in every few years and checking I haven't written anything that now feels ridiculously irrelevant or downright offensive. And you haven't got that with God, or Rumi, or Buddha, or Lao-tzu or Moses. Just saying.

So there's a very precise moment when Gaia and I realized that this profanity F**k It actually represents a 'spiritual' act, and could thus be a spiritual 'way' or philosophy.

It was September 2004, and we were nearing the end of our first summer running retreats at 'The Hill That Breathes', the retreat centre we'd created in Italy during the previous two years (having escaped London life in a camper van with our twin baby boys).

It was the final day of a retreat, and we'd likely have been teaching meditation, and some Chi Kung, and probably thrown in some Taoist philosophy.

And we ended with an exercise –

We were to give 'gifts' to each other in the form of a few choice words or sentences.

For example, one participant might have said to another: 'I give you the gift of courage to speak the truth to your partner.'

And there was one guest, an English woman living in Paris, who was exhibiting a malady we'd observed throughout that summer in the many guests who arrived on our Hill: she cared too much. She cared too much about what others thought of her, about how she was getting on in her career, about whether she was doing the right thing in the eyes of her parents, about whether she'd made the right choice to move to Paris, and so on.

And when it came to the time for me to give her a gift, I said something to this effect: 'I give you the gift of saying F**k It to everything that's concerning and worrying you. It really doesn't matter so much in the grand scheme of things; none of it. So say F**k It to all that and just enjoy yourself. You live in an amazing place, you have a great job, you're young and free… F**k It, live a little.'

She thanked me. The session ended. The retreat ended. Everyone went their separate ways.

Then, a week or so later, I received an email from her, saying that she'd enjoyed the retreat, loved the place and the food, but she'd been particularly affected by my gift of saying F**k It to her concerns, that she was now saying F**k It every day to this and that, and that she was feeling much better and freer and happier than she had for years.

Gaia and I sat contemplating this. Something was becoming clear. We had just offered, in a therapeutic context, a profanity – F**k It – as a therapeutic aid, and the client was now using that aid, to great effect, in her own life. This was quite something. No, it was more than something, it was really exciting.

We were seeing something for the first time. Because of our own total immersion, over the previous years, in the philosophies of the East, of Taoism and Buddhism, we could recognize something very familiar in this profanity of the West.

We saw that this one profanity contained, in a very Western, condensed and profane way, elements of letting go (of attachment), going with the flow, slowing down and relaxing… all critical elements of Eastern philosophies and practices.

And at that moment we wondered, therefore, whether we could teach F**k It as a whole philosophy; we wondered how deep this could go as an idea to share with people in a way that they could use for themselves as a therapeutic and spiritual tool.

So we put a week's retreat in the diary for the next year. The first 'F**k It Retreat'. We told a few people about it and they booked it. Within a short time, it was booked up.

Whenever anyone heard about the idea (i.e. of F**k It' as a 'spiritual way') they'd say 'great, yeah, I get that'. But getting something is different to feeling something and living something, and we were about to get our first testimonial for the power of F**k It.

The Healing Beginning

Around that time (September 2004), as well as sharing the power of meditation, and Chi Kung, and the wisdom of Taoism with people, and getting excited about the *idea* of F**k It as a spiritual way, I was feeling rather unwell physically.

And this was deeply upsetting for me. One day I was in our room on my own. We lived in two rooms of the retreat centre we'd set up. I was feeling pretty rough. And the background to my illness was that I'd suffered from allergy symptoms most my life. As well as effects on my lungs and skin, I'd feel generally under the weather, agitated and have trouble sleeping because of the symptoms. I'd noticed that my health improved on holiday, in a warmer climate, so one of the reasons we'd moved to Italy was the hope that my health would improve.

But after that first long hot summer, the driest and warmest summer my body had ever experienced, I was still unwell – if anything, more unwell.

I went from the bedroom into the bathroom and looked in the mirror at my ill-looking face. And I said, 'Unbelievable. We've done all this, all this work, borrowed all that money, dragged our young family out here, and here I am, just the same.' I felt a real sense of despair.

After a while, wallowing in this despair and self-pity, I thought, *Though it's not SO bad. I'm here with Gaia and the boys, my beloved family, in these Italian hills of paradise, with blue skies every day, hanging out with great people, teaching meditation and, well, I'm not THAT ill. F**k It.*

And as I thought those words, including the F**k It, I felt this huge burden lifting.

You see, I'd had this idea for years that I would only really be able to live my life once I was 'better' – i.e. fully well. And the language and ideas of holistic health supported this: to be well and holistic was to be 'whole'. So not to be well was not to be whole. And that's how I felt: not whole.

So for most of my life I'd been putting off living. So a lot was riding on this chance to finally *live*, because I'd been so confident that being in Italy would lead to my healing, my 'wholing'.

And here I was, in Italy, still ill.

So this moment of saying, 'F**k It, my life's okay, more than okay actually; I need to start living,' was very powerful. I was saying F**k It to the idea that I had to heal to be okay.

In that moment I gave up on the idea of getting 'better' and decided to live with how I was, just as I was. And it's hard to convey the sense of freedom I felt, especially now with this distance in time. But I was abandoning an idea (that 'I should get better') that, as well as giving me some hope in the gloom of illness ('surely I can get better'), was also burdening me and creating ongoing tension in my life ('why am I still ill'; 'how can I get better?').

So, 'F**k It,' I said. 'F**k It to the idea of getting better.'

And I began to live without that idea.

The thing is: within a week, I was feeling a little bit better.

Within a month, I realized I was significantly better.

Within six months, I was more well than I'd been in my entire adult life. In fact, I just felt 'well' and 'better'. Sure, if I'd eaten a nut I'd still have ended up in hospital. But I was experiencing no symptoms whatsoever.

And thus I became our first testimonial: I said F**k It and healed.

And, as I write this, I am still well, and have been well in all these intervening years.

From that moment, F**k It wasn't just an idea, it was even more than a feeling; I had embodied it so literally that my body had healed of illness.

I BECAME OUR FIRST TESTIMONIAL: I SAID F**K IT AND HEALED.

And if you're wondering what was going on? Well, you'll read a lot in this book about F**k It enabling a shift from tension to relaxation. And such a shift benefits every single area of our lives. Including our health. Eastern and Western medicines share the observation that stress is very bad for us. That it can contribute to or create disease. And even this word 'disease' points to this phenomenon of course: dis-ease, or lack of ease.

It can seem overly simplistic to say we need to relax to heal disease. But they've been saying and teaching this in the East for thousands of years.

And the more recent scientific studies done in the West are saying the same thing: reduce the stress, increase the relaxation, and healing happens.

And F**k It is the most powerful relaxation technique you'll ever find.

Thus… saying F**k It can lead to healing.

In the Beginning: Why Saying F**k It Is a Spiritual Act

When we say F**k It to things that are really getting to us (the things that are mattering too much) we do carry out a spiritual act. F**k It is the perfect Western expression of the Eastern spiritual ideas of letting go, giving up and relaxing our hold on things (attachments).

Of course, we could argue until the Second Coming about what 'spiritual' actually means. In a broad sense it's usually defined as the non-material: in whatever non-shape or non-form, but even this doesn't quite do it for me. I can get 'spiritual' feelings from the most material and everyday things. So let's not go too mad on an actual definition – it's enough to say that we probably both get what we're on about when we say 'spiritual'. And – in my experience – whenever we relax deeply and let go, we open ourselves to the spiritual.

WITH Fk IT YOU MOVE FROM ATTACHMENT TO FREEDOM.**

When you say F**k It to anything you move from tension and attachment to release and freedom. All philosophies, all religions, all spiritual disciplines offer the same promise: freedom.

The problem is that it's a very difficult promise to fulfil.

In fact, any philosophy that could fulfil that promise would be the ultimate philosophy... welcome to the philosophy of F**k It.

The problem for most of us in the Western world – stressed-out, uptight, anxious and controlling as we are – is that we need something with the power of an expression like F**k It to jerk us into a more relaxed state.

It also has the added advantage that it doesn't involve any of the following:

★ Praying

★ Chanting

★ Wearing sandals

★ Singing songs to acoustic guitars

★ Developing a belief that you're right and everyone else is wrong

★ Killing people

★ Eating beans

★ Wearing orange

★ Stopping yourself doing things that you want to do

★ Rules

★ Pretending to be happy when you're not

★ Saying Amen, unless you really want to

Amen.

The Beginning of Language: the Science of F**k (It)

In the early years of teaching the power of F**k It to groups on our retreats on 'The Hill That Breathes' in Italy, I would explain how this wonderful profanity works as follows:

We operate mainly, as adults, from the left hemisphere of our brain. That's where the language is, the logic, the working things out, the assessment of the past and the anticipation of the future.

Whereas when we operate from the right hemisphere, we're more present, relaxed, playful, creative and overall more peaceful. Things don't matter quite so much when we're in our right brain.

And saying F**k It creates a bridge from the left brain to the right brain, one that we can walk right over, and stay there for a while. And if we drift back to the left brain, we just say F**k It and go waltzing over that bridge again.

That was how I imagined it working. Because it feels like F**k It comes from the right brain. So when we use it in the left brain, it jumps us back to the right brain. Like magic.

Then, years after I'd been describing the effect of F**k It in this way, I read about a study of people who'd had damage to the left brain, and thus had trouble with speech. As these people could easily say swear words, however, the study concluded that, unlike all other language (which is generated in the left brain), swear words must be generated in the right brain, or across both hemispheres.

Which is beautiful. How I'd imagined it is close to what actually happens in the brain. The moment you say F**k It you jump from the left brain to the right brain.

This makes F**k It a unique tool in the English language. Sure, other swear words will create a similar jump. But it's the context that's important. We're saying F**k It to something that requires the shift in brain perspective. And thus we're recruiting that brain jump at precisely the moment we most need it.

The Beginning of a Whole New Genre

In 2006, when I started to approach agents and publishers with a view to getting this new book of mine published, I was pretty much laughed off the phone. One agent said, 'Do you honestly think a high street bookstore will put a book with the "f-word" in the title on their shelves?'

A year later, though, I was talking to Michelle Pilley and her team at Hay House. And they *did* have the vision to publish the book.

This F**k It book was the first book with 'fuck' in the title to hit the bookshelves of bookshops around the world.

Some years later, when other books arrived with 'fuck' on their covers too, the genre expanded exponentially.

And so, as you read this book, know that you're reading the *original* here; the progenitor of a whole fucking genre. You're going to the source. And that's usually where the spring water is the freshest.

Why F**k It has such a charge

*In that original edition, this is how I analysed the power of F**k It (before I knew it would make such a splash):*

It contains the word 'fuck'

A book like this is controversial simply because it contains the word 'fuck'. Funny, really. First because the philosophy behind this book is the truly anarchic thing, not the use of the word itself. But mainly because it takes a long time for a word to lose its power.

Yes, this word 'fuck' is truly beautiful.

YES, THIS WORD 'FUCK' IS TRULY BEAUTIFUL.

It's beautiful because it's slang for having sex. 'Fuck off' is really 'Go and have sex', which is not really an insult, more a good suggestion. 'Fuck you' is really 'Sex with you', which is certainly not an insult, more an invitation. 'Oh, fuck' is really 'Oh, great sex' – which, in your moment of frustration, is not a bad thing to be thinking about.

And this one word has the power to shock.

You can kind of understand why this was the case when the word was rarely used, when it was hardly heard in most circles. But in the 1980s and 1990s, it seeped and flowed into the language. It crossed barriers of class, race, and age as the expletive of choice. Its malleability is awesome: so much so that it can be used as *any* part of speech. Look at this:

'I thought, "Fuck this" (exclamation), when he fucking looked (adverb) at me like that, in his stupid fucking car (adjective), well, fuck (conjunction), I didn't give a fuck (noun), I fucking told him (adverb) that he was a complete fuck-face (noun) and that he could go fuck himself (verb).'

And the remarkable thing is that – even with this virus-like ability to spread – the word has kept a good deal of its power.

It's all about anarchy

Saying F**k It is like sticking two fingers up to the world of meaning, convention, authority, system, uniformity and order. And this is anarchy. Anarchy literally means 'without a ruler'. And anarchists do propose a state free from rulers and leaders. But the wider meaning of 'anarchy' is the absence of any common standard, purpose or meaning.

And this is the key to the anarchistic heart of F**k It. In life everything supports our relentless pursuit of meaning and the collection of numerous meanings. Even though meanings cause us pain, everything around us supports the process of collecting meaning.

In order to live harmoniously together we try to agree on standards, purposes and meanings.

So anything that threatens some of these collective meanings, the sacred cows of our semantic universes, is a great threat. Anarchism – the actual absence of meaning and purpose – is the greatest threat of all.

The narrower political connotation of anarchism – to overthrow the state – is nothing compared with the disruptive power of its true definition: to overthrow a common perception of meaning and purpose. In this sense, anarchism is the most disruptive and radical philosophy that mankind could ever dream up.

WHEN YOU SAY FK IT, YOU TAP INTO A PHILOSOPHY THAT SCARES THE LIVING DAYLIGHTS OUT OF EVERYONE.**

When you say F**k It, this is where you're going: you're tapping into a philosophy that scares the living daylights out of everyone.

So F**k It is loaded with two types of explosive: the word 'fuck' itself packs an impressive and offensive punch, while the phrase taps into the philosophy of pure anarchy.

And just before you get scared, stop reading and think, *I'm not interested in anarchy*, there's an interesting philosophical footnote hidden within the etymology of the word 'anarchy'. *Anarchos* (yes, this is all Greek, by the way) was a description often applied to God – to be 'uncaused' and 'without beginning' was considered divine.

This is a great moment. A moment when whole stadiums (or *stadia* if you know your Latin) of people should stand up and applaud and cheer. Here I am, writing about F**k It being The Ultimate Spiritual Way (which it is, by the way), and arguing that F**k It is in essence true anarchism, when I discover that God – GOD, no less – was referred to as *Anarchos*.

Holy Mother of Jesus, and Father as well, this is good news. Anyone would think there was a God guiding me through the presentation of His Ultimate Philosophy. But hey, God, I'm sorry, the whole concept of You is one commonly held meaning-thing that we anarchically have to say F**k It to.

Sorry, God.

How to Read This Book (Not Necessarily from the Beginning)

Most of you in the West will read this book from the beginning (front) to the end (back), unless you're one of those people more accustomed to reading celebrity magazines and prefer to flick through something from the back to the front. Just so you know, that won't help you with the ending (it's on the cover, anyway: F**k It is the Ultimate Spiritual Way).

But here's another great way to read the book (for those in the West or East): try opening the book randomly and see what turns up. It's like using tarot cards. Who knows how this works – but it does seem to. Have a go now just to confirm this (and surprise yourself).

Close the book.

Breathe deeply and focus on finding something that you need right now, today.

Then open the book randomly. Go on, do it. It's a great way to read.

TRY OPENING THE BOOK RANDOMLY AND SEE WHAT TURNS UP.

If you do this regularly and keep getting the same page, then it's probably still working: it's me telling you from a distance that you really need to focus on that area of your life.

Another great way to use this book is to read a chapter, then go out and tell people how much you're enjoying it, and how your life is changing by the minute. In this way you benefit yourself (good karma for spreading the word), others (who benefit from the message) and me (who's using all the proceeds from this book to build a house made of chocolate that I'll slowly eat my way through, then claim the full amount on insurance, saying it was termites, and start the whole damn thing again).

WHY WE SAY F**K IT

We Say F**k It When We Give Up Doing Something We Don't Want to Do

Every week, you clean the windows of your house/flat/barge. You do it religiously and conscientiously. But you're bored with it now. You do it because your mother always told you that clean windows say a lot about the owner. Someone with dirty windows, she thought, was probably dirty themselves.

But the pain of doing it every week has become so much recently that one Monday you just say F**k It and watch daytime TV instead, with a packet of chocolate biscuits. It feels great. As the weeks pass, you enjoy seeing the windows getting dirtier. They become a symbol of your new freedom. When it's getting difficult to see through them, you hire a window cleaner. You feel even happier with your new F**k It attitude when the

SAY FK IT AND WATCH DAYTIME TV INSTEAD.**

window cleaner is young and gorgeous… and you fancy bursting open a can of Diet Coke, so to speak.

When the things that we thought mattered to us start to give us pain, we can get to the point where we say F**k It. This is when we stop doing them and do something more fun instead. So:

* ★ We say F**k It to trying to get fit and watch the TV instead.

* ★ We say F**k It to being nice to people we don't like and ignore them instead.

* ★ We say F**k It to getting to work bang on time and try being late instead.

* ★ We say F**k It to the cleaning and get a cleaner instead.

* ★ We say F**k It to God and worship the Devil instead.

In fact, we say F**k It whenever we give up anything that is causing us some pain. We may say F**k It and give up being someone we don't want to be. We may say F**k It and simply give up caring about something we thought we should care about.

We say F**k It to obligations that don't suit us: from family, friends, work and society to the whole world out there. The pressure that everyone puts on us to be a certain way, and do certain things, just gets too much occasionally. And we say F**k It and do our own thing.

We Say F**k It When We Finally Do Something We Didn't Think We Could

So we finally do our own thing. For whatever reason, we stop ourselves from doing lots of things we'd like to because we think we shouldn't.

At this very moment, there are people saying F**k It and:

★ finally going over to the boy/girl they fancy and telling them how they feel

★ walking out of jobs they've had enough of to travel the world

★ finally speaking their mind to a friend or family member

★ taking a sickie for the first time in their career

★ speaking loudly in libraries

★ eating a whole chocolate cake

★ giving another driver the finger, then speeding away

★ lying on the grass, just staring at the sky for hours

This is freedom. Finally doing what you really want. Saying F**k It to the world and what people think of you and going for it.

This is the side of F**k It when you need an accompanying rock soundtrack. This is the stuff of those old Levi's ads: riding into an office on a motorbike, picking up the hotty and riding off into the sunset.

We Say F**k It Because Our Lives Are Too Meaning-Full

At the core of any F**k It utterance is our relation to meaning in our lives. The truth is, our lives are too meaning-full. Which is a nice cosmic joke. We tend to think our life's struggle is to find meaning: we want to find meaningful things to do; we worry about the real meaning of life; we worry about the meaningless. Yet it's the accumulation of meanings that causes the very pain that we end up having to say F**k It to.

3

We stopped cleaning the windows because the pain of cleaning the windows became greater than the meaning we attached to having clean windows (instilled in us by a parent).

We headed out on the highway because the pull of the open road finally overcame the meaningfulness of the structured career, mortgaged house and widescreen TV.

So let's look at the history of meaning (and pain).

How we fill our lives with meaning

Oh shit, look who's just turned up. It's the presenter of 'This Is Your Life' (Okay millennials and Gen Z, I'm talking about a TV programme shown in the UK and USA from the second half of the 20th century, in which someone famous would be surprised by the presenter, and then taken on a tour through their own life. You see what you've missed?). So the presenter has burst into the loo to catch you reading this book… or stepped onto your bus… or leapt out of the wardrobe in your bedroom to say: 'This Is Your Life!'

So up you get and make your way out of wherever the presenter has ambushed you. And we cut to the studio full of people from your life and a big screen at the back with a picture of you on it. Then you appear with the presenter, as if they'd constructed the studio right next door to your house. And we're off: You were born in 1965 to Jean and Derek Mayhew… etc., etc.

But this is you. So go back to the date *you* were born. And let's join you as you emerge gasping for air from the beautiful, dark warm place where you've been hanging out for the last nine months. What a bloomin' shock… all those bright lights and people… and there's no liquid to float around in; just space, just air.

Here you are. You've entered a space that has no meaning to you whatsoever. And that – at this point – is of no concern to you either. For a while now, you're going to be happy with simple meanings: mother's breast means food and drink and, well, mother's breast means food and drink. All the people gawping at you and making funny noises mean nothing.

The meanings of things grow naturally. And they're normally related to simply whether these things cause us pleasure or pain. The breast is pleasure. Funny feeling in our belly is pain.

The presenter now turns the page to a picture of you at the age of four; you are playing. Can you remember what it felt like then? Can you remember the pleasure you took in the simplest things? You'd watch raindrops fall down a window pane. You'd go outside and look up into the sky and feel the rain on your face. You'd adore the smell of the rain on the dry concrete. Sometimes you'd get an idea that you wanted to go somewhere else or do something else. But generally you'd be happy exactly where you were: immersing yourself in the texture of everything around you.

The meaning of things had developed: lots of things gave you pleasure and some gave you pain. And you were now pretty conscious of what those things were, to the point where you'd sometimes try to replace some of the painful things with pleasurable ones. And as you flick through the pages of your life now, looking at photos of you as a teenager, the natural search for meaning continues.

By now it means something to us to have friends and be liked by people; to have people around that fancy us; to have people around that love us; to be doing well at school or in sport or playing a musical instrument.

And our world of meaning becomes more sophisticated: sometimes it's about just having fun; sometimes it's about other people approving of us; sometimes it's about getting fulfilment from something we're doing; sometimes it's about helping other people.

And as we flick through the pages – through college, through our first job, through relationships, maybe through starting a family – we see the tapestry of meaning that makes up our lives become more and more elaborate. Or, like a scout who accumulates badges on his arm, we slowly but surely add to the list of things that mean something to us.

And this – for most people – is life.

And – most probably – This Is Your Life.

WE ACCUMULATE MEANINGS LIKE A SCOUT ACCUMULATES BADGES.

We create a life of things that have meaning for us: things that matter. Or you could say that these things are our values: they are the things that we value in life.

The better an employee we are, the more our job matters to us.

The better a partner we are, the more that relationship matters.

The better a citizen we are, the more other people's welfare matters.

The better a human being we are, the more our effect on the environment matters.

Things matter. And for most of us, things matter big-time.

Everything in society confirms that things should matter… so we never question it. But as we move through life, the list just gets longer and longer. So, as the presenter rolls his bandwagon of reflection into the present, have a look at what matters to you.

You can probably tick off a good few of the following things that matter:

★ how you look: whether you look too fat or too thin or too old or too young or too short or too tall

★ how successful you are in what you've chosen to do with your life

★ the people around you: family, partner, friends

★ making a difference with your life: by helping other people or doing something that changes things for the better, or doing your bit to try to save this planet we're on

★ money: simply having enough, or getting to the point where you have a great deal

★ getting the bills paid

★ having a good holiday every year

★ being honest

★ doing the right thing whenever you can

★ being reliable

★ having a laugh

★ trying to do something with your life

★ God/Buddha/Muhammad/Tao, etc.

★ your health

* finding your true self

* finding your life purpose

* finding inner peace

* getting to work on time

* meeting deadlines

* setting a good example

* not swearing in front of the children

* speaking your truth

* having time off

* the gardening

* music

* being there for people when they need you

And, of course, we could continue the list forever. Because there are infinite possible meanings in this world… infinite potential for things to matter.

So, for one moment, compare the list you have now with that image of yourself as a four-year-old. Phew, the responsibilities of adult life, eh? Practically without realizing it, you've created for yourself a whole convoy of things that matter.

EVERY SINGLE THING THAT MATTERS EXPOSES US TO THE ELEMENTS OF LIFE.

And every single thing that matters exposes us to the elements of life. Everything that matters to us is like having a plan for life that we expect life to stick to.

But life has other ideas.

So no matter how hard we try to stay healthy, we sometimes get sick.

No matter how much we want to protect the ones we love, they're sometimes hurt and in trouble.

No matter how hard we try to get to work on time, sometimes we get delayed and we're late.

No matter how much we try to do the right thing, sometimes we get drunk and do the wrong thing.

No matter how much we want to be liked, sometimes we're not… no one calls us and we feel terrible.

Sometimes life has other ideas about one of the things that matter to us.

Sometimes life has other ideas about a few of the things that matter.

Sometimes life has other ideas about the whole bloody lot.

The bigger our convoy of things that matter, the more likely it is that life's going to mess around with our plans for it.

Meaning is pain

Anything that has meaning for us – anything that matters – carries the potential to cause us pain. Meaning is a brightly coloured box with pain inside. And sometimes – without us wanting it to – the lid just bursts open and the pain comes pouring out.

MEANING IS A BRIGHTLY COLOURED BOX WITH PAIN INSIDE.

The problem is that meaning – things mattering – is attachment. And anything that we're attached to has the potential to turn round and bite us.

The Buddhists do a big thing on attachment. And you can see why. It's their equivalent of sin. Freedom from attachments takes you a good way down the road to total liberation. In fact, it may well be the road itself. And the hard shoulder. And all the service stations along the way. And maybe even the Portaloos in the lay-bys, though I'm not entirely sure about that last bit. That may be pushing it a bit far.

Here's the rub, though – you try dumping your attachments. Dumping all your desires. It's not easy. No, that's like saying running a mile in a record 30 seconds is not easy. There's a darn good chance it's not possible. Ever.

But anyway – on with the argument – I don't want to get you down too much. Not yet, anyway. Enough to say for now that meaning in whatever form is attachment. And attachment carries some form of tension. When meaning goes, the attachment goes. And so does the tension.

Perspective teaches us about meaning

You might remember this from a Bond movie, or maybe from one of those magazines that told you how life would be in the future (and of course, it never has been): picture a man standing upright, holding on to two bars, then taking off and flying around. Jet propulsion for one person. You pull back a lever, open the throttle and you're 100 feet up.

Let's call this your Perspective Machine.

We're wandering through the woods of life, looking at the trees. And the trees are all the things that matter to us. Some we like the look of, and we take care of; others fall down right in front of us. Some even fall on us. Because things sometimes go seriously wrong. Terrible things do happen to us, or around us. Someone close to us dies; we're involved in an accident; we find out we have a serious illness, and so on.

When these things happen, the Perspective Machine goes flying up through the trees into the sky. And all the things that mattered so much to us, we can hardly see from up here.

For example, someone who discovers they have cancer suddenly can't understand why they were worrying about so many insignificant things before: the in-tray at work; managing to pay their taxes; the fact that they'd put on some weight over the last few years.

In one instant, all the things that really mattered so much suddenly matter very little or not at all.

Hanging up there in the Perspective Machine, you can still see the trees down below, but they're now so much smaller. And now that you can see all of the woods and the fields around, you realize those trees are pretty insignificant.

GIVEN PERSPECTIVE, ALL THE LITTLE THINGS SEEM PATHETICALLY IRRELEVANT.

With the news of 9/11, 7/7 or one of the tsunamis, or when the global pandemic hit, most of us went shooting up in our Perspective Machines. Suddenly all those little things that we'd been so preoccupied with in our lives seemed so pathetically irrelevant. We were alive and our family was alive. And that was all that mattered.

Anything that sends our Perspective Machines up into the air – from personal tragedy to world tragedy, to seeing something that really makes us think – is just like saying a big F**k It to all the normal concerns in our lives:

'F**k It, what was I worrying about?'

'F**k It, I need to really live and stop getting stuck in these little things.'

'F**k It, I'm going to help people and make a difference.'

Of course, we could also go through a thought process that takes our Perspective Machine up into the stratosphere.

It goes something like this:

I am one person among 8 billion people on this Earth at the moment. That's one person among 8,000,000,000 people. That's a lot of Wembley Stadiums full of people, and even more double-decker buses (apparently, these are the standard British measurements for size). And we live on a planet that's spinning at 67,000 miles per hour through space, around a sun that's the centre of our solar system (and our solar system is spinning around the centre of the Milky Way at 530,000 miles per hour).

I AM ONE PERSON AMONG 8 BILLION.

Our solar system alone (which is a tiny speck within the entire universe) is very big indeed. If Earth was a peppercorn and Jupiter was a chestnut (the standard American measurements), you'd have to place them 100 metres apart to get a sense of the real distance between us.

And that's just space.

Have a look at time, too. If you're lucky, you'll get around 85 years on this Earth. Humans have been around for 300,000 years, so you're going to spend just 0.0283 per cent of human history living on this Earth. And humans' stay on Earth has been very short in the context of the life of the Earth (which is 4.5 billion years old): if the Earth had been around for the equivalent of a day (with the Big Bang kicking it all off at midnight), humans didn't turn up until 11:59:54 p.m.

That means we've only been around for the last six seconds.

A lifetime is gone in a flash. There are relatively few people on this Earth that were here 100 years ago. Just as you'll be gone (relatively) soon.

So, with just the briefest look at the spatial and temporal context of our lives, we realize that we're utterly insignificant. As the Perspective Machine lifts us up so far above the woods that we forget what the word means, we see just one moving light. It is beautiful. A small, gently glowing light. It is a firefly lost somewhere in the cosmos. And a firefly – on Earth – doesn't live for long. It glows beautifully, and then goes.

A LIFETIME IS GONE IN A FLASH. THERE ARE RELATIVELY FEW PEOPLE ON THIS EARTH THAT WERE HERE 100 YEARS AGO. JUST AS YOU'LL BE GONE (RELATIVELY) SOON.

And up there so high in our Perspective Machine we realize that our lives are really just like that of the firefly. Except the air is full of 8 billion fireflies. They're glowing beautifully for a short time. Then they're gone.

So, F**k It, you might as well REALLY glow.

Fk It, you might as well REALLY glow.**

And there we go again. Did you taste it? That was the brief taste of freedom. Sometimes it doesn't last long. But it's an unforgettable taste.

Personally, I've always tasted it when I've contemplated the utter meaninglessness of my own existence. It's a rush of freedom and it tastes good. If my life means so little, then F**k It, I might as well go for it and just have a laugh.

What happens when the meanings become too much

We're about to take the Perspective Machine so far up into space that it just dissolves, like sugar in a hot cup of tea.

It may never happen to you, but sometimes a life crashes. And it can be like one of those spectacular crashes from a '70s thriller, when the car goes straight through a barrier on a corner that happens to be on the steepest slope you've ever seen, and the car smashes against the rocks and crumples up, then bounces down the slope, smashing into more pieces as it goes until it lands in the canyon below, a smashed-up heap. Then there's a pause. Then it bursts into flames.

This could be started by one of the big things that we've talked about before: one of the things that normally give you a good deal of perspective. These things don't always cause lives to crash, however; people have stayed sane through the most incredible trials and tragedies. But lives do normally crash when some of the things that people have placed a lot of meaning on go very wrong.

And lives also crash for no obvious reason.

When a life crashes, you – and those around you – know about it. It's not a lesson in perspective. It's not a lesson in anything. It's just a deep dark void of despair. It's when people think they're hitting rock-bottom and they just keep going.

I experienced a crash of sorts myself. It wasn't so much a smashing-down-the-rocky-slope crash as a serious prang, but it was one of those that will give you whiplash injuries bad enough to keep an osteopath's children at private school for a day a week at least.

Let me set the scene of this everyday collision. It was 2002, and we'd been wandering around Europe for months in a camper van with barely a care in the world. The summer seemed to last forever. Especially as we were still on the beach and swimming in the Adriatic in southern Italy in late October. But the time came to return to London and make a few pennies before our next outing (whenever that might be).

We drove into London on 5 November: Guy Fawkes Night in the UK. This is usually a day of mild excitement for me, given the prospect of exploding dynamite, writing your own name with sparklers and getting bits of tin foil in your teeth after eating a jacket potato. But within three days we had gone from sun, sea and surf to the dark, drizzly, grizzly streets of south London. That, plus the prospect of having to work, and my rapidly failing health, sent me into a big downer.

The following night we were arguing about how to get some bloody futon out of the van and into our new home, a tiny south London flat, when I lost it. I pulled the camper van across the traffic and came to a halt; half the camper van was on the pavement, the other half across a lane of traffic.

I got out and just went to lie down in the gutter.

Given the considerable amount of rain that was falling every hour, the gutter was more like a river. I lay there and curled up like a little boy and started moaning.

And that was the high point of the week.

For the first time in my life, I lost all sense of meaning. I hated being alive. Every single moment I felt in pain. When you're in pain, normally you can escape it in some way. Even if it means taking very strong painkillers. But the horrible dawning truth for me was that this was one pain I could not escape, because it was simply the pain of being alive.

Well, of course there was a way to escape that pain too… by not being alive. But although I could really understand why people take their own lives, it wasn't something I seriously contemplated.

Gaia was supportive. But for a while I was well beyond help.

We went to a workshop together. She assured me that it would be a 'safe space' to be myself, and for people just to listen. As we were on the Underground, nearing the north London destination of the workshop, I started to feel something I'd never felt before. I realized that I was so down… that so little mattered to me… that I really didn't give a shit what anybody thought of me. And this was amazing. I didn't care what the other passengers thought of me as I hung my head and sobbed occasionally.

As we got to the comfortable north London house to join the workshop, I realized I did not give a foetid dingo's kidney what any of these polite people thought of me, either. And this felt very new for a man who *did* care what people thought of him… throughout my life it had mattered to me very much how I was seen.

So I used this safe therapeutic space to the max. In the usual 'share' at the beginning, some people opened up and cried a little. And everyone felt for them, and put an arm round them. And previously in workshops like that I might have cried a little and everyone would feel for me, put an arm round me and give me a hug.

But I blabbed like a baby.

No one could touch me. Nothing would help. I was at the centre of a beautiful therapeutic exercise that really should have worked for me. But I was in the same empty, dead and dull space afterwards as I was before. And I learned something about therapeutic groups: the patience for people in a difficult place is not that deep… especially if the therapeutic methods on offer don't seem to have an effect. People were actually getting pissed off with me for being so darn down. And I didn't give a shit about this either.

And I still remember that new feeling I had that day. In the dark despair of the living pain I was feeling, I could also feel a freedom I'd never before experienced in my life: it was the freedom of nothing mattering. In my nihilistic gloom I was just saying F**k It to everything.

The dark cloud passed and I slowly returned to a 'normal' view of life. But something stayed with me: that feeling that things really didn't matter like they used to. Or rather, I'd lost something that never came back: the feeling that everything matters so darn much.

In the following years I read a good deal of spiritual literature. Well, in fact, that's all I read. I read everything I could get my hands on about Taoism, Buddhism, Shamanism… and all the colours of New Age Spirituality. I read everything from the most influential contemporary teachers. And something started to strike me reading about these modern teachers: that many of them were telling their personal story, and that they were very similar… they were all about the crashes that they'd had in their lives.

I REALIZED THAT THINGS REALLY DIDN'T MATTER LIKE THEY USED TO.

So please step forward: Brandon Bays, Eckhart Tolle and Byron Katie.

Brandon Bays – after years of working in the healing field – was devastated when she found she had a large tumour. Yet she achieved an astonishing and rapid self-healing. But 18 months later, she was hit by a series of terrible blows. Her beautiful house in Malibu was burned to the ground. Then all her income was taken by the IRS, so she had no money in the world. Then her adored daughter Kelley, her 'soul mate', wrote saying she didn't want to have anything to do with her any more.

And, finally, her husband revealed he'd been having a relationship with someone else. Bang. In the middle of this, she woke up: time stood still and she decided to trust. She was immediately bathed in a total feeling of love – a feeling that love was everywhere.

Brandon Bays 'woke up' and later created the inspiring book, *The Journey*.

Eckhart Tolle lived – until his 30th year – in an almost constant state of anxiety and depression. Then one night –

> *I woke up in the early hours with an absolute feeling of dread. I had woken up with such a feeling many times before, but this time it was more intense than it had ever been... Everything felt so alien, so hostile, and so utterly meaningless that it created in me a deep loathing of the world.*

At that moment, his 'deep longing for annihilation, for non-existence', popped and turned into something else. He had an insight about existence – about the 'self' that he was having trouble living with – that stopped his mind completely. When he came round, his perception of the world was transformed. He saw the beauty in everything and he lived – moment to moment – in peace and bliss. Eckhart Tolle 'woke up' and later created the bestselling work *The Power of Now*.

Over a 10-year period, Byron Katie's life slowly spiralled down. She descended into depression, rage and paranoia. At times she couldn't leave the house or even bathe or brush her teeth. Her own children would avoid her through fear of her outbursts. Finally, she checked into a halfway house for women with eating disorders. There, she was separated from the other residents because they were frightened of her.

Soon after, as she lay on the floor, she woke up with no concept of who she was any more. 'There was no me,' she says. She felt only joy and acceptance. When she returned home, everyone thought she was a different person. Byron Katie 'woke up' and later created the beautiful work *Loving What Is*.

Now, all three ideas/processes have a great deal of merit. But there's something missing, isn't there? Going deep into your emotional layers (*The Journey*) and living more in the now (*The Power of Now*), or asking yourself four questions about what pisses you off (*Loving What Is*) have got diddly-squat to do with what joins the three together:

★ They all had major crashes in their lives and then something happened.

★ They all said the biggest F**k It they'd ever said and then something changed.

So shouldn't they be teaching that? Shouldn't that be the process?

I know it wouldn't be quite as bestselling, but shouldn't the process really be about having some major crash in your life?

So you've signed up to the Crash Your Life, Say F**k It and Wake Up course. It's cost you £10,000 for the one-month course. Our team of specialists is ready to crash your life:

★ Our impersonator calls your boss and pretends to be an employee of a competitor... and claims that you've been passing on confidential information to them for serious cash.

★ Our thief has transferred £5,000 in notes into your desk drawer that morning.

★ Our Robert Pattinson look-alike then starts following your wife and manages to 'accidentally' bump into her. Within three days your wife is called away on a last-minute business conference. And the business, of course, is Pattinson-alike.

★ Our hacker uses the details you gave for your direct debit to us to hack into your bank account and steal all your money.

★ Our identity thief wipes your name from both the deeds of your house and the registration document of your BMW 5-series.

★ The court takes over your house.

★ You're now left with (practically) nothing and no one, and as you sit on the kerb outside your (ex) house, our martial artist mugs you and grabs your Rolex.

★ At this stage – although we make no guarantees – 78 per cent of clients say F**k It. And five minutes later they wake up.

Job done.

But seriously, this is obviously not something I'd recommend. So don't blame me if you bring on some kind of life-crash and it doesn't work. It means you're just a silly beggar. And if silly beggars ever wake up, they're still silly beggars, so why would you want to go and do that anyway?

What I *do* recommend is using the spiritual process of saying F**k It to start releasing your hold on all those meanings that have the potential to cause you so much pain.

PART 2

ESSENTIAL F**K IT
TECHNIQUES

These five techniques will help you to live a F**k It life. In fact, I recommend that you tattoo the techniques onto your fingers. That way you won't forget them. Give it a nice flowing typeface – though I wouldn't italicize it or you might end up looking a bit 'country restaurant'.

As you may well soon observe, the techniques flow into one another and depend on one another. And that's a bit like making a fist with your tattooed fingers: ready to smash your uptight life into submission.

And F**k It is the knuckleduster of this fist. The more you say F**k It, the easier it will be to use these techniques. And the more you use these techniques, the easier it will be to say F**k It.

Relaxing

Most of us don't know how tense we really are. Not you? You're actually really relaxed? Okay, let's see.

As you're sitting reading this, begin to focus on your shoulders: you can probably feel them dropping as you relax them. Then move to the neck, feel the tension dissolving away. Then go to your jaw: let the jaw feel slack as you relax it. Then the forehead and the muscles around your eyes.

Now go back to your shoulders. The chances are they've tightened up again: so try to relax them and let them drop once more.

And this is how it works. We find tension where we didn't think there was any, and as soon as we move our attention away the tension returns. It can be a little disconcerting when you first get into the habit of going into the body consciously like this, because your impression is that you're actually quite tense (whereas before, your ignorance was a peculiar form of bliss).

If you ignore tension in your body, though, it does what children (and some adults) do when they're ignored: it starts shouting, screaming and generally misbehaving. This misbehaviour takes the form of aching necks, headaches, backache, etc.

So have a go at listening to your body *before* it starts to shout for your attention.

Remember that we're very simple beings, too: we tend to try to avoid pain and increase our own pleasure. So far we've been talking about avoiding pain. Try also, then, to find pleasure in relaxing. Try to find as much pleasure in relaxing as you would in a glass of wine, a kiss with your partner or _____ (please insert your favourite pleasurable activity here, though do be a tad careful in case someone else picks up this book after you; I don't want the expression of a pleasurable activity to become, ironically, painful for you).

I call this 'internal pleasure seeking'.

Now some smart-arse once pointed out in a workshop I was teaching that *all* pleasure is internal. Well, yes, of course.

But I'm talking about finding the source of pleasure inside you rather than outside yourself. This usually wouldn't cross our minds. We desperately try to stimulate internal pleasure (otherwise, yes, known as 'pleasure') through an external search. Again, write the things that tickle your fancy in the margin (if we fill this book with too many spaces it will become too much like a workbook and I hate those, or we'll get letters from people saying, 'I bought your book expecting some meaningful advice and all I got was lots of spaces. Next time I'll buy some blank paper from the stationer's: it's a lot cheaper.').

If you can find the source of pleasure inside yourself you'll never be bored: you'll be self-sufficient and you'll become a very cheap date, too. But the biggest boon is that if you can find pleasure in the very thing that can boost your own health and lead to a long life, happiness and possible enlightenment, then you're a damn sight more likely to do that thing on a regular basis.

FIND THE SOURCE OF PLEASURE INSIDE YOURSELF AND YOU'LL NEVER BE BORED.

So go on, retire to your room, shut the door and do a bit of internal pleasure seeking. And after you've done that, try to find some really deep pleasure in simply relaxing. Start to enjoy what it's like to take a deep breath. Enjoy the feeling of your hands tingling as they relax more. Get turned on by your whole body feeling as mushy and slushy as ice cream melting on a hot summer's day.

Letting Go

Maybe it's because we innately know that everything is impermanent that we so desperately cling to it. But cling we do. We know that our youth vanishes, that we and our loved ones will die one day, that whatever we've accumulated can easily be taken away from us, that one day our skills might not be wanted, that a day may come when our love might not be reciprocated. Yet we go on clinging.

Everywhere we turn we are faced with impermanence. I'm writing this in early October, and as I look outside I'm faced with nature's yearly reminder that everything fades away.

Of course, the more we cling, the more pain we feel as things fade, disappear, or die around us. And sometimes the more we cling, the more these things happen. Imagine someone in a relationship who is, yes, clingy. They hold on to what they think they love with an iron grip, are jealous at the slightest thing, spend their time in fear of what terrible things might happen rather than enjoying the relationship as it is. How does that make the other person feel? How long does that relationship last? (Bad. And not long. Just in case you were sitting there scratching your chin, wondering.)

The key to being able to let go of all the stuff you're holding on to is knowing that you'll be okay if you don't have it. And that's the truth. This is a good exercise: go through all the things that you really want to hang on to in your life – the partner, the job, your health, your sense of humour, your family and friends, the soaps on the TV – and tell yourself that you would (actually) be okay without them. You can survive with very little. And though the passing of people and things can be painful, you will survive.

If you're up for it, say this to yourself a few times: 'I am okay with things passing and fading away in my life. I will be okay no matter what happens to me and those around me. I let go of my hold on life and allow life simply to flow around me and through me.'

Now light a candle and burn off your own eyebrows. Noooo. Don't just do what I say.

But do relax (finger 1), let go (finger 2) and get ready to accept (finger 3) everything as it is.

THOUGH THE PASSING OF PEOPLE AND THINGS CAN BE PAINFUL, YOU WILL SURVIVE.

Accepting

Are you aware how much people around you moan (and, okay, maybe you and me too – eek!)? This is why we moan and bitch and criticize: because we don't feel so good inside, and we try to find reasons outside ourselves for this discomfort. But as you start to feel better inside (by saying F**k It, by relaxing and letting go), you'll get to like the feeling it gives you, and you won't find it as easy to moan about everything. After a while you'll positively dislike doing it, because it'll make you feel worse, not better.

You'll find that it's best to try to accept things around you just as they are (and this will be easier as you lose the need to justify your own painful feelings). The truth is (I'm sorry to break this to you) that there's usually diddly-squat we can do about most of the things in our lives that piss us off. We can't do a great deal about litter, late buses, high taxes, incompetent politicians, young people swearing and being disrespectful…

Even stuff closer to home: your boss being a buffoon, your partner being selfish, your children being lazy. Sure, you can leave your job, and your partner, and kick the kids outside to do a bit of good, healthy exercise. But until you're ready to do these things, stop bloody moaning and accept things as they are.

And we've all had great practice accepting difficult things that we can't control throughout the pandemic. It started off with having to stay at home for a few weeks, then months. And the path of the pandemic this far in (and as I write this, it's 18 months since the first lockdown in the UK) has meant that every aspect of our lives has been affected: how and where we work, meeting our friends and family, shopping, travelling – there's nothing that hasn't been affected. We've become so much more adaptable. And, I have to say, I've heard a lot less moaning about any of the measures than I would have expected. People, I think, have recognized the absolute seriousness of the threat, and got their heads down, stayed in, and generally accepted this huge change in their lives.

Accepting everything, just as it is, is a beautiful state to get to.

Take your practice from during the pandemic and feel it now: what would it be like to accept yourself just as you are, not slimmer or better-looking or funnier or kinder, but just as you are right now? What would it be like to accept your life just as it is: job, family, friends, sex life, prospects, the whole bloomin' lot, just as it is right now? And what would it be like to accept the world – fucked-up, messy, warming up, pandemic-sensitive, war-strewn, greed-littered – just as it is?

Try it today. Accept the things that don't go according to plan, the people who don't treat you quite how you'd like to be treated, the bad news as well as the good. Start to enjoy feeling good inside yourself. And remember that you don't need to moan and criticize any more. And if you do feel crap inside (like we all do sometimes), try to accept that feeling, too, without looking for things outside yourself to blame it on.

Watching Impartially

The Watcher is not some creep sitting behind almost-drawn curtains, spying on the neighbours. No, it's what those of us who sit behind drawn curtains on cushions meditating call the ability to watch what goes on in your own mind and body impartially. This is sometimes also referred to as 'consciousness' or 'awareness'. But let's stick with The Watcher.

Sitting still for a little while (which is usually rather off-puttingly referred to as 'meditation') is a good opportunity to get in touch with your inner Watcher. Do you see how giving your Watcher that capital 'W' has already given them some importance in your life? Sit there and, as the thoughts start to roll in – as they invariably will – develop a sense of watching the thoughts (from above if you fancy), as if they're not yours. Don't get involved with the thoughts. Don't judge them. Just accept them.

Try imagining The Watcher as a CCTV camera on a busy high street. The camera sees everything. It doesn't intervene or shout out, 'Hey, you, big nose, you look ridiculous in that jacket.' It just watches. In fact, the chances are that there's no human being watching a screen of big nose and his jacket. The camera is just a piece of dumb machinery watching (and most probably recording, just in case). A camera watching, not judging or criticizing.

And do you know the effect of this little bit of inanimate machinery? People behave themselves more. And that's pretty much what happens in your mind/body, too. The more you watch impartially – accepting what is seen just for what it is – the better your mind/body is likely to behave. It doesn't have to behave better, of course: there's no MI5/NSA going to be looking at the footage of your thought crimes. But the truth is that when you accept your thoughts and feelings just as they are (through The Watcher), then everything tends to slowly calm down a bit.

Have a go and see for yourself.

And if you're having trouble with it – with getting some distance between you and your thoughts/feelings – have a listen to this. We were living in a small flat in Balham, South London years ago. Every night I'd sit cross-legged in silence for half an hour (at around midnight). The flat was part of a huge block, so you could hear the noises of humanity being human at all hours: toilets flushing, doors slamming, TVs blaring, babies crying.

As I settled myself, and my mind began to slow down, I slowly became aware of voices next door. They were male voices, maybe two people, just chatting away about the usual inane day-to-day stuff. I could just about hear what they were saying if I concentrated hard enough. And I remember feeling a little surprised that they were talking like this – so audibly – at this time of night. I listened a little more. I contemplated that I'd never before heard people talking next door: I knew there was a middle-aged man living there alone, but I'd never heard him with anyone else.

And I listened.

Then I realized with a jump that the voices weren't next door at all: they were in my own head. I was listening to my own thoughts (as inane and day-to-day as they usually are) as if I were completely separate from them.

I tried to tune in again. But the spell had been broken. I was astonished. I really had been convinced that these voices were coming from next door. I understood (maybe for the first time) that I am *more* than my thoughts. I understood that there is something else – in my head, or elsewhere – separate to the thoughts that I'm having.

Some people would say that I had – at that moment – merged with the source, or with God or the universal being. I have no idea. But it felt good. I've not tried to replicate the experience since – but I have had similar glimpses occasionally, usually when I'm driving.

As you develop The Watcher in you – your own CCTV camera – you get that slight sense that the thoughts are just happening, and that you don't have to get into them. Don't shout, 'Eh, big nose', just watch the colourful passing crowd of your mind with total impartiality.

JUST WATCH THE COLOURFUL PASSING CROWD OF YOUR MIND WITH TOTAL IMPARTIALITY.

Conscious Breathing

Conscious breathing is very easy, yet very powerful. So for the increasingly lazy and carefree F**k It practitioner, there's not a lot to do or think about.

Breathing is a marvellous thing to play with. For most of us breathing is something we don't (and don't have to) think about, ever. After a difficult painful first few breaths when we're born, we tend to breathe pretty well for the rest of our lives without thinking about it.

Of course, if we have asthma or any other lung condition, we'll be very conscious of our breathing. But for many people, the only time they think about their breathing is if they feel sick and they're told to 'take some deep breaths (and put your head between your knees)' by their mother.

Breathing is one of the miraculous automatic functions of our body: like the pumping of blood from our hearts, the exchange of oxygen and carbon dioxide, the regeneration of cells, the digesting of foodstuffs, the clearing of toxins, the balancing of acidity and alkalinity, and so on.

Our bodies just get on with their own business without us. And that's all very good. It would be a bummer to wake up in the morning and to have to go through a checklist of what to do:

* Breathing? Check.

* Heart pumping? Check.

* Correct hormones releasing? Check.

* Oxygen to carbon dioxide ratio 2:1? Check.

* pH level 7.4? Check.

* 20 per cent cells regenerating? Check.

* Engaging right side of brain? Check.

* Release adrenaline to begin worrying about the day? Check.

Now, here's the point. And it's a big one. Of all these numerous functions that are going on automatically all the time, breathing is the one that we can very easily play with and change.

Sure, if you really put your mind to it, you can slow your heart rate down. But it ain't that easy. Whereas now, sitting where you are, reading this, you can breathe more deeply, or more quickly, or you can hold your breath. And everything that you do consciously with your breath will have an effect on the rest of your body (and mind).

That's why Conscious Breathing is so cool.

If you sit and breathe consciously and deeply now for a few minutes, you'll feel calmer, and a whole bunch of things will start to happen in your body:

★ Your heart rate will slow down.

★ You'll send more blood into your internal organs.

★ You'll send more oxygen to your cells.

★ You'll probably be releasing less adrenaline and cortisol into your system.

★ You'll send a message to every cell that says, 'Hey, relax a little, it's not so bad after all.'

There are two sides to Conscious Breathing: bringing consciousness to how you are breathing now, and changing your breathing consciously.

Simply bringing consciousness to how you are breathing now allows you to get to know your breath. And it's a good idea to start doing this. Sure, as soon as you start to think about your breathing, it changes a little bit. It's hard to really catch it by surprise and see what it does when you're not looking. There's no dark wardrobe you can hide in and peek out of to see how you're breathing when you're not looking. Your lungs always know when you're in the wardrobe – no matter how small the crack is that you're looking out of.

But have a go. Notice what the breath feels like as it enters your nose (or mouth). Notice what moves when you're breathing. Are you breathing into your chest or belly? Are you breathing quickly or slowly? Are there any pauses in your breathing? Can you feel the effect of your breathing in other parts of your body? Concentrate on your hands: is there anything going on in your hands as you breathe in and breathe out?

Notice how you breathe when you're relaxed. Notice how you breathe when you're in a big meeting at work, or when you're with your lover. Get to know your breathing: how it works, and how it changes. Start to learn your patterns and your ways of breathing. This is the first side of Conscious Breathing. The second side is to start playing with the breath – changing your breathing and breath patterns and seeing what happens within your body.

It's worth knowing a little bit about how our breathing works.

The inbreath is (obviously) when we take things in and expand. We take oxygen in. We take energy in. And our body expands with this. The chest or the belly expands, but so does the rest of the body, too. When you really get to know your breath and body, you'll feel the expansion in every part of your body.

The outbreath is when we let things out and we relax. We let out carbon dioxide. We let out tension from our body. The whole body softens and relaxes and drops a little when we breathe out.

A little word on the 'energy' here. You might have lots of experience with energy, but you also might have no idea what I'm talking about. Energy – aka *chi*, or *qi*, or *prana*, or life-force, or life energy – is what they go on about a lot in the East, and what we have pretty much ignored here in the West.

First off, energy exists. It's not some esoteric idea. It exists and it is life. If we had no energy in our bodies, we'd be dead. Energy is a moving, tingling, magnetic-feeling force that moves through our bodies (and the form of anything else that's alive). Chinese medicine is all about the balancing of this energy to create a balanced physical system.

For now, if you know very little about this energy thing, simply be open to the possibility of feeling something new in your body. Or maybe starting to put a name to something you've already felt. The best time to spot this energy thing is when you're really relaxed. First, because – when you're really relaxed – energy flows. Second, because being relaxed will give you the space to feel the energy properly.

A little warning, though: beginning to feel your own energy can be seriously addictive. It feels gorgeous. It's like being bathed in light. It can feel ecstatic just to be sitting and feeling this life-force buzzing around your body. You can get hooked on this feeling and want to find

A LITTLE WARNING: BEGINNING TO FEEL YOUR OWN ENERGY CAN BE SERIOUSLY ADDICTIVE.

ways to increase it. (But there are no side effects to this addiction; you will only feel better and get better.)

And the best way to increase the feeling of *chi*, of course, is to say F**k It to everything, and breathe.

Conscious Breathing is the perfect aid for the F**k It practitioner.

The F**k It Outbreath

Let's start with the F**k It Outbreath. If saying F**k It is about letting go of the things that matter and create tension, then breathing out slowly is the best way to help this process. That's what the outbreath is: you release what you don't want; you let out all the waste gases and toxins and tensions that are not welcome in your body.

The quickest way to relax is to really slow down the outbreath. Really drag it out. And start to feel your body relaxing. You can exaggerate the effect of this even more if you add a sigh to the outbreath.

The sigh is an amazing tool in itself. You sigh when you're at the end of doing something difficult and strenuous. When you've finished work and poured yourself a whisky and you sit down on the sofa to watch an episode of your favourite show, that's when you sigh. Sighing says to your body, 'That's it, you can relax and let go now.' Sighing is your way of saying, 'F**k It. No matter what's been going on today, now is my chance to sit back and relax.'

So if you want to trick your body into thinking that all the work's been done, and it can just sit back and relax, then SIGH.

Have a go at combining some F**k It thoughts with some sighing outbreaths. Choose whatever you want to say F**k It to at the moment, speak it out, and then have a long, sighing outbreath. A quick warning here again: if you're reading this somewhere public, it may be best if you wait until later, when you're on your own. Or maybe just tone it down a bit... mumble your F**k It line, and then breathe out slowly. I'm sorry, I just don't want to get you into trouble.

Try it.

'I say F**k It to my bad back.' Then sigh and breathe out.

'I say F**k It to my rude boss.' Then sigh and breathe out.

And so on.

Whenever things matter too much. Whenever you feel tense or anxious or afraid. Just say F**k It, then sigh and breathe out. It works a treat.

JUST SAY F**K IT, THEN SIGH AND BREATHE OUT.

The F**k It Inbreath

But let's not forget the F**k It Inbreath. While the F**k It Outbreath is about letting go and relaxing, and saying no to things, the F**k It Inbreath is about pulling in energy and strength, and saying yes to things.

The F**k It Inbreath is about sucking in the energy to do what you want to do. And this is at least half the game in leading a F**k It life. If you want to get up from your desk and go and chat with the dishy new account director, take a deep breath, say F**k It, and do it. If you want to go travelling, take a deep breath, say F**k It, hand in your notice and go book your flights. If you're tired of your boring relationship, take a deep breath, say F**k It, and end it. Today.

In energy terms, the F**k It Outbreath is yin… relaxing, soft, letting go.

Whereas the F**k It Inbreath is yang… energetic, enthusiastic, embracing.

And if you know anything about Taoism, you'll know that you need a good balance of yang and yin to live harmoniously in this world.

The problem for most of us is that we live somewhere in between a good yanging and a good yinning life. So we don't go for things enough, we don't embrace life as vigorously as we could. And we don't relax and let go enough.

This is replicated in our breathing, just as everything in our lives is replicated in our breathing. If you look at anyone's outbreath and inbreath, they can look quite similar. The F**k It Inbreath is full of energy, though – try it, really fill up and pull in the energy. And the F**k It Outbreath is exactly the opposite. There should be no effort in letting the air out, just a letting go and relaxing.

The two breaths could not be more different. And each breath offers you the two sides of living the F**k It life.

Start practising breathing like this. Enjoy the active sucking-in of energy that is the F**k It Inbreath. Then enjoy the absolutely passive letting-go that is the F**k It Outbreath. And you'll start to enjoy how this impacts on your life, too.

You'll give yourself the F**k It energy of the F**k It Inbreath to really go for it in life: to do what you really want to do, no matter what other people think.

And you'll give yourself the F**k It ability of the F**k It Outbreath to really not give a fuck about things that used to bother you and get you down.

So now let's look at how we can say F**k It in specific areas of our lives.

PART 3

SAYING F**K IT

Even Your Own Mind Will Resist Your Impulse to Say F**k It

'Oh no it won't,' you say.

'Oh yes it will,' I say.

'Oh no it won't.'

'Oh yes it bloody well will.' Oh, I'm sorry, there are children present. Oh well, they shouldn't have come to a pantomime called *F**k It* anyway.

If your mind is anything like mine, it resembles a bad pantomime. And I have Piers Morgan playing Cinderella's Fairy Godmother in my head, which makes it all the more fascinating a place to be.

Your head may be nothing like a pantomime, of course, but one thing I know for sure is that it will resist any impulse you have to say F**k It.

What the mind does

Knowing what your mind gets up to is a fun game. You see, once you know what's going on in there, you know what you're taking on, because the mind is often seen as the enemy.

We meditate (sometimes) in order to watch our thoughts and calm them down. We develop 'The Watcher' (maybe) in order to get some blessed detachment from the rabbiting of the mind. We become 'conscious' or 'aware' (if we're lucky) so that we're not simply controlled by what happens in the mind.

And remember, the 'mind' here is something more than the functioning brain. It's the thoughts we have; it's the feelings we have; and it's the receiving and processing of our senses: 'sensations'.

If you could watch your thoughts for just 30 minutes, you'd be amazed at what you saw (and heard).

I usually can't be arsed to do exercises, but if you have a mind that likes them, a good one to do is to write stuff down when you wake up. Just leave a pen and a notebook next to your bed, and once you've woken up (yes, you can have a pee if you want to, but you don't need to clean your teeth, not just yet), start writing.

Just write whatever comes into your head. No one is ever going to read it (if you don't want them to), and it's a good idea if *you* don't read it either, for a few days at least.

Just write whatever you are thinking. If you stop thinking, then stop writing. But when you think something again, just write it down. If what you're thinking is this: *Ooh, I'm really hungry. I don't know what to have this morning... corn flakes or sugar puffs? Ooh, shall I invite the honey monster into my stomach... what do you think, honey monster? Tell 'em about the honey, mummy! Yes, honey he said, but if it's honey, why do they call them sugar puffs? Should have called them honey puffs. Shit, I'm hungry. I wonder if I could stop writing and eat something? Shit, I'm tired, too – I must stop looking at porn into the night,* that's fine, just write it all down.

Do a week's worth and then have a little read through. You'll find that on the days you do it you'll tend to feel better than usual during the morning. This is because writing all that stuff down is a bit like having all the silly thoughts in your mind scraped out for a while.

The mind has a kind of addiction to the fears around the things that matter – an addiction to the negative. A lot of us moan and gossip about other people, and it creates a real and peculiar pleasure in us. Even if people have harmed us, the moaning about it creates this subtle pleasure in us.

In the relentless comparison with, and judgement of, others, when people do anything that we don't approve of, it gives us pleasure because in some way we feel superior to them.

THE MIND HAS AN ADDICTION TO THE FEARS AROUND THE THINGS THAT MATTER.

The possibility of saying F**k It to any of the things that really matter is, then, anathema to the mind. If you say F**k It and recognize that these things don't really matter, the mind has to give up its struggle, its resistance, its negativity, its judgement, and its constant moaning. And the mind is not going to give up these things easily.

Even though they create misery in you, there's pleasure locked somewhere inside them: like a mint humbug, every hard and miserable emotion and feeling has a soft, delicious, chewy centre for the pain-obsessed mind.

Say F**k It, Yes

You know the kind of thing:

It's not really you, or the sort of thing that a person like you would do, or you feel scared that you might fail or make a fool of yourself, that you might be exposed, because it's out of your comfort zone, and you haven't really got the time anyway, and maybe it's better for someone else, not you, and you're not sure if you're quite ready for it yet, that you're too young, or maybe you're too old, or you have to think about the kids, or your partner, or your parents, or the money, or the time, or the phase of the moon, or the fact that you're not so well, or that you're actually fine so why would you need that, and and and…

You say no.

When you could have said yes.

Life's often about knowing which to say, when.

Or, rather *feeling* which to say, when.

And when you're being pulled towards a no, when you could probably do with saying a yes, then F**k It is REALLY going to help.

Say 'F**k It, yes.'

And if you need to 'yes, please.'

Say F**k It, No

You know the kind of thing:

You should really do it, of course, it's what you do, and people expect you to do it, don't they, they'd be let down if you didn't, or how could you resist an opportunity like this, some people aren't lucky enough to get opportunities like this, it's the natural step on, it's what you deserve, it'd be rude not to, they'd be offended, it's what your partner wants, or your children want, or your parents want, it's what the world wants of you, you need to do your bit, you need to go for it, just do it, don't look a gift horse in the mouth, get out of your comfort zone, they would, wouldn't they, if they got half a chance and and and...

You say yes.

When you could have said no.

Life's often about knowing which to say, when.

Or, rather *feeling* which to say, when.

And when you're being pulled towards a yes, when you could probably do with saying a no, then F**k It is REALLY going to help.

Say 'F**k It, no.'

And if you need to 'no, thank you.'

Say F**k It and Do What You Fancy

Having sat here at my desk, eating a bowl of Weetabix (other wheat biscuits are available, and, I've noticed, significantly cheaper), I took a few deep breaths, relaxed, and tried to get a sense of what I fancied writing about next. Something, that might make you, dear readers, think *Wow, that's a whole approach to living in itself, and I could start doing that NOW.*

And then (just now) it came to me: why don't I write about how to – on a regular basis – sit still, take a few deep breaths, relax and try to get a sense of what you'd fancy doing next. And then do it.

WOW, THIS IS A WHOLE APPROACH TO LIVING IN ITSELF, AND I CAN START DOING THIS NOW.

Which I'm now doing, thus demonstrating the last essential stage of this deceptively simple approach to living a more fulfilling life.

I could end this chapter now, because those are the steps. But if you don't understand why this is so powerful, you probably won't give it another thought and you'll just carry on with your habitual pattern of not doing what *you* fancy, and be more likely to do what other people fancy you doing.

And that would be a crying shame – literally a 'crying shame' – because most of us, at one point or another, when our lives are led by the needs, desires and requirements of others, end up crying about what a shame it is.

So here goes – strap in for some 'understanding':

Fk It** You tend not to do what you fancy. You tend to do what you think you 'should' be doing or what someone else wants you to do or what your 'to do' list informs you is the next thing to do. And I can hear the hundred reasons you have for justifying this approach, but think about it: you're spending your precious days on this planet *not* doing what you fancy. Oh dear. Time for some refining.

46

Do Even though this loaded two-letter word is next in our sentence, it's actually the final, critical stage of our plan. Once 'what you fancy' has been established, you must *do* it. Otherwise, you're just a dreamer. Otherwise, there's a constant gap between what you fancy and what you do. And that's even worse than not doing what you fancy, but not really thinking about it.

What This is the critical tuning-in bit. It's necessary to take a few deep breaths and relax first. Otherwise, you'll experience interference around knowing what you truly fancy. But once you're relaxed, open your full senses to this 'what' (you fancy) and listen carefully. The message will be there. Just wait until it arrives.

You Yes, you. Not what everyone else fancies you doing. But *you*. Not the parents or the kids or the partner or personal trainers or friends or neighbours or society or companies or advertisers or advice gurus or priests or books or anything or anyone else. You.

Fancy It's got a more louche, racy air to it, this word, than, for example, plain old 'want'. But even if the object of your 'fancy' isn't obviously racy, it has that feeling when you're doing it instead of something you feel you 'ought' to. I could sit here now, and take a few deep breaths, and relax, and ask myself what I fancy doing next. And the answer might be to get up and go to the supermarket. If I 'do' that, then it'll feel rather racy and radical. To be wandering around the aisles of a supermarket whilst I 'should' be finishing this chapter (and writing more) – ooohhhh, you are naughty, Mr Parkin.

Fortunately, what I fancy doing next is finishing with these few, hopefully persuasive, words: if you were to take JUST this simple process from this book, and do it many times a day, to the point where it becomes natural, your life would change. How could it not?

You'd sear a new pathway into your brain. Gone would be the 'do what I should do' pathway. And there would be the 'F**k It, I'll do what I fancy' pathway, lying ahead of you in all its glory.

Sit still. Take a few deep breaths (relax). Ponder what you fancy next. Do it.

Say F**k It and Binge-watch

Last night, I had an evening to myself. The world was my oyster.

I could have gone out. I could have had a meal out. I could have gone to the cinema. I could have walked along the promenade listening to the waves crashing onto the beach, or enjoying the skateboarders and buskers and ballroom dancers in seaside bandstands that is Brighton beach of an evening. I could have met up with friends. I could have driven to Devil's Dyke and looked across the South Downs under the light of the moon. I could have written some more chapters of this book. I could have cooked up a new idea for another book. I could have lain in a hot bath listening to meditations or educating myself with one podcast or other.

But I didn't.

At 6 p.m., I moved from my desk to the sofa and picked up where I'd left off in the current multi-series Scandinavian *noir* that I'm watching. And, apart from trips to the loo, the kitchen and to answer the front door, I didn't get up off the sofa until 1 a.m. Seven hours of watching the same programme on the TV.

When I wondered about food, I ordered a takeaway (that was the trip to the front door).

When I wondered about drink, I filled up my glass (that was the trip to the kitchen).

When I felt tired, I nodded off for 20 minutes.

I was aware that I should really be getting up and going for a walk. But the more I stayed, the harder it was to move.

And I was SOOOO comfortable, stretched out on the sofa, I couldn't have been more relaxed.

And I was SOOOOO enjoying the detective drama. So well written. So intriguing. So need-to-see-the-next-episode.

And I SOOOOO enjoyed my Chinese food takeaway. Every lazy MSG-filled mouthful was delicious.

> **SAY F**K IT, GIVE IN TO THE BINGE-WATCHING IMPULSE WHEN IT TAKES YOU AND SEE WHERE YOU END UP.**

Yes, I was SOOOO lazy. Seven hours of binge-watching.

But today I was up at 7 a.m. writing new chapters for this book.

It's hard to yang if you haven't yinned.

There's no up if there hasn't been a down.

It's hard to be on if there hasn't been an off.

So, F**k It, give in to the binge-watching impulse when it takes you and see where you end up.

Say F**k It and Ask for What You Want

So you're saying yes to things you'd normally say no to, you're saying no to things you'd normally say yes to, you're doing more what you fancy, including binge-watching the TV, now it's time to ask for what you want.

There's a good chance you're not great at asking for what you want. Especially if you're great at generously giving people what they ask for (whether partner, family or friends, work colleagues or the world in general).

The roots of our hesitation in asking for what we want (and need) in every area of our lives lie in how we were nurtured as a child. If we were lovingly nurtured, given what we needed and our requests were listened to, then we probably feel safe asking for what we need in life. For the rest of us, if that wasn't the case, it means that we don't feel safe asking for what we want or need.

It's likely that we're afraid we'll be rejected if we ask for what we want or need. Because this is our fear from childhood. When we are young, the love of our carers is everything to us, so if we pick up any hint that our desires and needs are not respected, then we tend to remain quiet and not ask.

Because this pain is so deep (if I ask for something you might reject me), we have to consciously go out there and, step by step, start asking for things. We have to learn that we won't be rejected and abandoned if we ask for something. Sure, there will be times when people say 'no'. But they're unlikely to abandon us.

So start asking.

Start with the small things. Ask for a change to the pizza toppings on the menu: be polite, but ask if you could add one thing to the toppings listed on the menu (and my Italian family would say that that should never be pineapple, but I say bring on the pineapple, what can't be improved by the addition of some pineapple?).

Ask someone to do you a favour. In situations where you'd typically compromise or remain silent, ask for just how you'd like it.

This does of course, take a F**k It or two. This is a F**k It to the fear that we might be rejected and abandoned. But the more we ask, the more we learn that it's okay to ask, and the less we'll have to say F**k It and grit our teeth as we ask.

And what about a wider, broader asking for what you want too?

You know the thing: asking life, the universe or a deity.

I'd say: F**k It and have a go. Whenever I've been very clear about what I'm asking for in my life (and I'd probably talk about 'the universe' as many would these days), the results have been spectacular and beautiful.

All we have to do is ask.

And by asking, the stars seem to line up and provide us with wondrous things.

We just need to remember to be clear about what we want, and ask.

ASKING FOR WHAT WE WANT TAKES A FK IT OR TWO TO THE FEAR THAT WE MIGHT BE REJECTED AND ABANDONED.**

Say F**k It and Listen to the Signs

When we get better at listening to ourselves (and what we fancy), another type of listening emerges too.

And I'm going to call what we start to hear 'the signs'.

In fact, the writing of the original version of this very book was an essential part of the story that's an object lesson in listening to the signs (yes, I'm writing this chapter years later).

I was, at the time, exploring deeply how it would be to follow my own way more, and listen to any subtle signs out there: a form of deeper listening in and out.

I was travelling back to Italy from the UK, and about to catch a train to the airport. I had a feeling that there was something wrong about the train, but still got on, knowing that I was going against this strong feeling (and even though there would be another train 15 minutes later that would still get me to the airport on time).

I'd ignored 'the signs' so the signs decided to put on a show for me.

Within 10 minutes, the carriage I was in was filling with smoke. I raised the alarm and the train stopped and a small fire (amongst litter) was extinguished underneath the carriage I'd chosen.

The train limped on to the next station. I ignored the signs (for a second time) that I should now get off. The train continued towards the airport but hit a flood on the track. And had to reverse back to the station. This time I got off. I caught a bus to the airport instead.

When I reached the airport (now rather late), I had a choice: to queue for my booked flight (with others from the bus), but risk not getting on in time. Or take another queue to get on a later flight that day. I could feel the pull towards getting in the queue to find another flight. So, this time, I listened to that pull, that sign. And I got the last alternative seat into Italy that day. I also discovered that I would have been turned away from my original flight as we would have been too late.

I used the hours that I now had spare to do a final check on the draft that became the original version of this book.

The signs are often subtle (even if they made themselves loud and clear in that case, in their fire-and-flood biblical proportions). They're like subtle markers on our paths – markers of warning or encouragement that we can heed or ignore. In fact, most of us don't even notice them in the first place. The noise of everything else that we're paying attention to is just too loud. That's why the calmer listening in seems to go hand in hand with this calmer listening out.

There is, of course, nothing new to the idea that there are subtle signs out there for us to listen to if we care to. Even in our language, we have two words that reveal the two sides of this art: 'ominous', referring to that sense we get when things just don't feel right, that something bad is going to happen; and 'auspicious', the opposite feeling, that this is a good sign and that we should carry on down this path.

THE SIGNS ARE LIKE SUBTLE MARKERS ON OUR PATHS THAT WE CAN HEED OR IGNORE.

And why F**k It in this case? Because it's so easy to dismiss such signs. It's so easy to think that we're being irrational or superstitious or over-sensitive or fearful. So we have to say F**k It to our tendency to dismiss such feelings and signs.

Of course, we do need a rational internal discourse too. And we need to be able to distinguish between natural fears and an unusual, uncomfortable feeling or sense of dread. Like anything, it takes practice.

And the first step in your practice is to look out for the signs in the first place. Because they're everywhere when you start to look.

Say F**k It to What Other People Think of You

Over the years, we've often asked people, 'What do you most need to say F**k It to?' And the most common answer has always been: 'What other people think of me.' So it's time to say F**k It to what other people think of you.

Why we care about what other people think of us

Some of us care a lot about what other people think of us. And it seems a very basic urge as we're growing up to seek approval. I saw it when my children were young: they loved to be seen doing things, to be laughed at when they did funny things, to be congratulated when they did something special. If we give children the attention and the approval they are seeking, they tend to develop a sense of self-worth or self-esteem. In other words, by fulfilling their need for approval from the outside world, they tend to develop a sense of self-approval.

WE ARE DEFINED BY THE LEVEL OF SELF-APPROVAL THAT WE HAVE.

And it seems that, as we grow up, we're defined by the level of self-approval that we have. If our earlier need for approval wasn't fulfilled and we therefore have a low level of self-approval (please feel free to interchange the word 'self-esteem'), then we're likely to continue wanting approval from the outside world.

If a loving environment in childhood created high levels of self-approval, then we're less likely to be constantly seeking approval from others as adults.

Of course, between these two extremes lie most of us. We're not rabid attention-seekers, but we are also sensitive to how people view us.

The other aside here is that I have no particular judgement about this either. It's a subject that has always fascinated me. Particularly in regard to success. Those with low self-approval can be driven to high levels of success because of their exaggerated need for the external approval that they probably never got as children.

Imagine the hyper-driven, mega-successful film or pop star who appears to have endless energy for new roles, and new ways with which to woo an ever larger world audience. Think of someone like Marilyn Monroe. She had the world at her feet. She even had the president of the world's superpower at her feet (well, maybe not her feet), yet she's famous for her insecurity, self-doubt and lack of self-approval.

Go the other way and a young adult with high levels of self-approval might lack the drive to 'achieve' anything — they're content to just bumble along, enjoying life.

We care, then, what other people think of us: first of all because we want their approval; more so when we lack approval for ourselves.

We're also taught that it matters what other people think of us. We're taught that to live successfully in society, we should be respectful to other people, we shouldn't upset anyone, we should help people, and we should do as we're told (to take an example of a very early teaching that we receive).

WE'RE TAUGHT THAT IT MATTERS WHAT OTHER PEOPLE THINK OF US.

We learn that it matters what other people think of us because that's how everyone else is. That's how your parents probably were, that's how your teachers were, that's how your friends were.

Another reason it matters to us what other people think of us is that we tend not to know what we actually want. If a person has a very clear aim and goal in life – for example, to play soccer for England – they tend to get on with fulfilling this goal no matter what. Because they know what they want, and are confident in achieving it, they have the strength to deflect all the different critical views that come their way: you must spend more time doing your homework; you must think about doing a proper job; you're just a waster... etc. When we know what we want, what people think of us can become less important in the pursuit of that goal.

The iffy side of caring what other people think of you

Caring what other people think of you clearly works for some people. For others, it constrains and narrows their life. If you're surrounded by safe, conservative people – and you care what they think – you're unlikely to move beyond the safe, conservative boundaries that they place on their own lives. No matter how you feel – no matter what your desires – you will feel blind fear at the thought of doing things that upset those people around you:

★ This is how LGBTQ+ people end up in straight marriages.

★ This is how talented singers end up as accountants.

★ This is how comedians end up as barristers.

★ This is how people happiest on the open road end up in blocks of flats.

We all have bundles of potential. And the iffy side of caring what people think is that you might well end up doing only the safe things that they want you to do. Everyone simply imposes their own fears and regrets on everyone else: when one person limits themselves, they can be certain to go around limiting other people (usually in a very moral fashion) to try and make up for the deep pain they feel for not doing what they should have done.

Which brings us on to…

Other people are rarely being personal

When you really care what other people think of you, you tend to take everything personally. It's possible to develop a somewhat twisted view of the world when you really care what other people think. You crave approval, and when you get it, you're happy. When you're the life and soul of the party, or the centre of attention, you're happy as Larry (I'm not quite sure which Larry, but let's hope he was a happy fellow, otherwise that bit won't work).

But something that smacks of anything but approval throws you off.

If someone neglects to say 'Good morning' to you, you wonder why. If you aren't lauded for your new report, you get down (I don't mean in a funky way, but in a depressed way). If that attractive woman/man doesn't look at you, you start to wonder whether you're ugly. A shop assistant is rude and off-hand to you and it makes you furious. A car cuts you up and you chase after them, in the mood to kill.

Your somewhat paranoid view of the world – where you start to take everything personally – can become ridiculously exaggerated.

I know people whose whole life revolves around fighting back against the rude and ignorant people (strangers) around them.

So it may be that the person who neglects to say 'Good morning' to you is being personal: they may well not like you. But it's very unlikely that the person cutting you up on the motorway has singled you out for some rough treatment because they don't like the look of your face.

But the truth is, even those who from almost every perspective seem to be being personal with you, are not being personal. They're probably venting their own negative emotions. It may be that you mirror their shadow-side: the part of them that they can't admit to. It may simply be that they're jealous of you for some reason. It may be that they're simply in a bad mood and just want to take it out on someone.

But the fact is that practically every time someone gets personal with you, it's almost always more about them than it is about you.

So it's not worth taking anything personally, because it's unlikely to be about you. Of course, if you weigh 20 stone and you go and sit on your neighbour as a joke and they start to suffocate and splutter, 'Get off me, you fat bastard, you're going to kill me, you lardy moron,' then it *is* personal, it *is* about you, and they *have* got a point. And I'd get off them and go home and make yourself feel better by eating a tub of Häagen-Dazs in front of *Flashdance*.

IT'S NOT WORTH TAKING ANYTHING PERSONALLY, BECAUSE IT'S UNLIKELY TO BE ABOUT YOU.

You can't keep everyone happy

If it really matters to you that other people approve of you, y͟ invariably come up against one hell of a bummer fact: you can't please all of the people all of the time.

It's a fact. No matter how much you bend over backwards for people, you'll always disappoint people, upset people and downright piss them off sometimes.

This is because everyone is different. Every single person has a unique GFUC, or Genetic Fucked-Up Code. Most people are fucked up, but their fuck-ups are completely different. Which means that – even with one person – as much as you try to please them, you're going to tap into one or two of their fucked-up qualities and get some kind of stick for it.

The fact is that – even when you really want to – you can't keep that many people happy for that much of the time. That's because people aren't that good at being happy. And they're not that happy to simply 'approve' of other people. They prefer to find things in you that piss them off… things in you that they think are inferior to the things in them… this makes them feel (temporarily) a little bit better.

But – if you care what other people think – it makes you feel terrible.

Do you want to make everyone unhappy?

If your early attempts to get approval from parents and the people around you failed big-time, there's a chance you'll be mightily pissed off. And this tends to really hit the world when you're a teenager.

You've spent so long wanting people to like you – without anyone saying anything nice to you – that you decide to hit back. This is you saying to the world: 'Okay, I wanted your attention. And if you're not going to give it to me for all the good things I did, then you'll bloody well give it to me now. You'll not be able to ignore me, you sad bastards. Because now the bomb is going to go off.'

This is when things go pear-shaped. This is when boys and girls and men and women cause havoc and end up achieving their aim: they get attention.

And they end up making everyone scared and unhappy. All they're doing is asking for love… it's just got a bit messed up along the way.

So, by talking about caring less about what people think of you, I don't mean growing a mohican, spraying 'Police are wankers' on your dad's car or setting light to the church hall.

It's worth thinking about how much you care about what other people think of you, not least because the moment you start to say F**k It to various things in your life, you'll really start to wind people up. And it's worth being ready for this.

SAYING F**K IT TO THINGS WILL REALLY WIND PEOPLE UP

Before you started reading this book, you were involved in a conspiracy of meaning with everyone around you. You and they gave the relatively usual meanings to various things in your life: you will have had shared experiences of what mattered. You also fit perfectly into your place in the world: your parents expect you to be one thing, and expect certain behaviours (related to how you view different meanings), so do your friends, so do your colleagues at work and your boss, and so does the rest of the world, including the government (it continues to expect that a person like you regards it as important to pay taxes, for example).

The moment your world of meanings starts to shift a little is the moment you start to upset this balance. The moment you start to free yourself from your normal attachments and meaning by saying F**k It to things, is the moment people will start to get pissed off with you.

This is because all the other people around you, deep down, know that their myriad meanings are the cause of all their problems. It's okay to stay within this pain when everyone else is doing the same thing. But as soon as you show that there's possibly another way, they'll get very jealous. Something deep in them will see the freedom they've always craved and they'll want it. But they won't come politely to your door or desk and ask you if you could be so kind as to share whatever wisdom you've received; they'll kick back and criticize you and think you're terrible.

This is because anyone who shows any signs of real freedom reminds everyone else what a prison they're living in. And prisons, especially nowadays, seem to be darn difficult things to get out of.

YOUR FREEDOM REMINDS EVERYONE ELSE WHAT A PRISON THEY'RE LIVING IN.

We've had numerous clients over the years who've made the leap to freedom and upset those around them who are stuck in their own prisons:

★ The ones who left marriages and relationships that weren't working and infuriated those around them stuck in marriages and relationships that weren't working.

★ The ones who gave up great careers for a simpler life or to go travelling and faced the wrath of those chained to the career ladder.

★ The ones who said no when everyone around them thought they should say yes.

★ And the ones who said yes when everyone around them said no.

Let's say that you've really examined your feelings and issues around death, and that death now holds less weight for you. In many senses you've said F**k It to death. Death means less to you. When someone close to you dies, you go through some grief that you can't spend time with them any more. You remember the good times you had together.

But this lasts a relatively short time. And you are soon back to normal life. Those around you, and your family, think your behaviour is strange and callous. You don't get involved in the drama of the death. You haven't fulfilled the expected quota of grief demonstration.

And people criticize you.

The fear of death creates an expectation of reaction. If you don't fulfil this expectation, you will be criticized. In the end, people simply take it personally: 'Well, you don't really seem to have cared that much about this person; is that how you feel about me? Is that how quickly you'll forget me once I've died?'

When the power of a meaningful world begins to diminish for us, we challenge everyone whose worlds are still so meaningful. So the moment people do start to react to how you are, smile and say quietly, F**k It.

It's time to say F**k It to what people think of you.

Approval is like anything else in this life: it can cause pain if it has a lot of meaning for you – if you're attached to it.

This is not to say that if people are prostrating themselves at your feet and telling you how wonderful you are, you shouldn't enjoy it. But if you believe you won't be happy until every last damn citizen of this planet is worshipping you, then you're in for a hard time.

So start saying F**k It to what people think of you.

If you can be arsed, you can do a little exercise:

Speak out (or write down) what you think other people think of you, and then follow it with a big F**K IT:

★ My mum thinks I should get a proper job. F**k It.

★ My dad thinks I should settle down. F**k It.

★ My boss is threatened by me. F**k It.

★ God thinks I'm a hopeless sinner. F**k It.

It really doesn't matter what people think of you. Just like nothing really matters.

★ Enjoy going your own way.

★ Enjoy zigging when others are zagging.

★ Enjoy doing something in public you wouldn't normally do (this is not an invitation to flash, by the way).

★ Enjoy telling someone the truth for a change rather than just trying to keep them happy.

★ Enjoy being rude to someone who pisses you off.

It's time to care less about what others think of you.

It's time to say F**k It and feel what it's like to be free.

Say F**k It to the Ups and Downs

This is the small print on any financial investment literature:

'The value of investments may go down as well as up. Past performance is not a guide to future performance and may not be repeated.'

That is specified to counter an element of natural human psychology: that when we see something going well, we tend to think it'll continue to go well; that what has happened in the past will tend to be repeated in the future.

So potential investors tend to see the ups and assume they will continue. Then get shocked by the downs.

In life, then, as in finance:

Things can do down as well as up. What's happened in the past is not a guide to what might happen in the future.

But in life, as in finance, we don't see the downs coming. And we're shocked by them.

So, just as investors do, we need to say F**k It to the idea that it will always be 'up' and that the future will repeat the past.

Life always has its downs as well as its ups.

We also need to say F**k It to the idea that it will always be 'down' and that the future will repeat the past.

Life always has its ups as well as its downs.

Not a lot you or I do will change that (and what I mean by that pithy 'not a lot' there is that of course we do have some influence on our ups and downs, but not full control).

So here's what the up and down game involves:

When things are up, be grateful, but remember that it probably won't last forever, and be even more grateful for what you have and what you're going through.

When things are down, when you're feeling down, fully feel those feelings. Don't try to hide. But remember that it probably won't last forever, and you'll be back on the up sooner or later. It's natural to be on the down, and to feel down, occasionally. The more you can sit with those feelings, as reality, the quicker they move through you, and the reality changes.

And these four words will help you, whichever part of the up–down cycle you're on at the moment: THIS TOO SHALL PASS.

Say F**k It to Fear

Fear and love

There are two apparently opposing forces that govern our lives. No, not good and evil. Love and fear.

That's right: the opposite of love is not hate, but fear.

We tend to operate in either of these two modes.

THE OPPOSITE OF LOVE IS NOT HATE, BUT FEAR.

We either embrace and love life – this is called the *libido*. And I like this word. Mainly because most people think it's about how high your sex drive is. So when you say, 'Yes, I have a high libido,' they think you could be a sex addict and suggest you should be put in a dark room with Michael Douglas. But libido in its wider meaning is simply a love for life. If you have a high libido, you simply have a great love – even lust – for life.

And Lust for Life – as well as being a great song by Iggy Pop – is a great thing to have. When we go out to life with love, we are completely open.

The opposite mode is when we are in fear (rather than in love). In fear we close to life. In fear we go inside and hide. We want to retreat and block ourselves off from experiences.

Most of us are constantly moving between these two modes. It's a bit like a game of snakes and ladders. We bound up the ladders of love, sucking up life for all that it is. Then we hit scary snakes and slide down them as we retreat from life. It's a good analogy, because one thing that a lot of us are bloody scared of is snakes. Which takes me on to my next point rather neatly.

It is rational to be afraid of some things

There are things in life that it's understandable to be afraid of. A fear of snakes and spiders is quite natural, as – depending on where you are in the world – both can be very dangerous. If you

THERE ARE THINGS IN LIFE THAT IT'S UNDERSTANDABLE TO BE AFRAID OF.

hold some innate fear of a snake, then when you see one, adrenaline will start to pump and make you more able to act quickly and appropriately.

Some people have a 'fear' of blood. Again this is quite natural, because if we ever see bright red arterial blood, it means things are pretty serious.

The problem with even these very natural 'fears' is that they can get out of hand. A fear of blood can lead you to faint at the sight of blood rather than act quickly to stem its flow.

I prefer the idea of being aware around dangers rather than being scared. And this is indeed what *beware* means… to *be aware*. It's important to be aware of how dangerous driving a car is, but not to be scared of driving. It's helpful to be aware that crossing a busy road carries a risk, but not to be scared of crossing roads. It's wise to be aware that skiing down a black slope in a blizzard has potential problems, but not to be scared of skiing.

As I write this during a global pandemic, this process of 'being aware' has become particularly difficult. In order to become aware of the actual risk to us, we've had to become armchair experts on statistics, probability and risk analysis. Unlike at any other point in my lifetime, literally leaving that armchair and going out of the front door has carried a more palpable risk and one that's also been more difficult to assess.

For the first time in my life, agoraphobia – the fear of leaving our homes, or entering open or crowded spaces – has been the most rational response to the situation. In fact, it has been in the interest of public safety to, in some way, induce a level of agoraphobia. In the deepest of lockdowns, without police patrolling the streets (as they were in, for example, Italy), it's been the fear of infection (or of infecting others) rather than the fear of punishment that kept us indoors.

And during the pandemic, for me personally, understanding and assessing the risks as accurately as possible has helped overcome the general (though not irrational) fear. In fact, I've never been more aware, or calculated so precisely, the risks I take when I carry out an everyday task, such as going to the supermarket.

The trick is, and will be, to keep up with the data and the facts as things change, and as the risks change and reduce. We've been living through an inversion of the aeroplane phenomenon: where, in normal times, an aeroplane, even though we know it's a highly safe form of transport, can feel risky and scary. In the pandemic, commonplace activities, such as going to the supermarket, which we'd normally consider safe and secure, have become riskier and scarier. What looks scary (flying in a metal tube) is actually rather safe. What looks safe (buying metal tubes from supermarkets) has actually been rather risky.

We have, therefore, been mucking deeply with our innate evaluation of risk. And that will take a lot of adjustment, and a lot of rational awareness of what the true risks are.

For the time being, if I'm about to get on an aeroplane, and am nervous about it, and you hug me to reassure me, it's likely that the hugging is far riskier than being on the plane.

In this pandemic, we've been reminded that it is very natural to be scared of things that have the potential to cause us pain, even death: and this is the origin of fear in us.

The origin of fear

'Fear' in us is not just one lump. It's a sackful of stuff that we've built up over our lives. And fear grows from the experience of pain. When we experience pain we – very naturally – do not like it and we do not want to experience it ever again. So the experience of pain then becomes a fear.

FEAR GROWS FROM THE EXPERIENCE OF PAIN.

For example, we might be quite happy chopping up carrots with our favourite sharp knife every day. Until the day that we take the end of a finger off. The pain creates a fear of using sharp knives. We have just added another bit of fear to our sack.

You might be quite happy speaking in meetings at work. Until the day that you're feeling a little bit under the weather, and – halfway through making some brilliant point – you completely lose your track. You stumble and fall. You have no idea what you were saying. And apologize and fluff your way to a halt. It's embarrassing beyond belief. And the pain stays with you for the rest of the day. Come the next important meeting and you suddenly find you're afraid to talk. One more screwed-up ball of fear for your sack.

The problem with life – as we now know – is that anything that means something to us has the potential for pain. So it's possible to develop fears for anything and everything. Some people are scared of falling in love because of the pain they've previously experienced in love. People are scared of doing what they want to do because it previously went wrong for them. Some people are scared of leaving their own house because of some pain they previously experienced outside the house.

Let's not forget that this process is natural. Even the apparently extreme expansion of the fear sack is quite natural. It's based on a principle that we all take part in: feeling pain and then being scared.

This is why age often brings with it a heightened sense of fear. Time for some people simply offers more opportunities to experience pain and develop fear. This is one reason why older people can be very scared and timid.

Yet we all know people who seem to be absolutely fearless. They are adventurous and confident and are out in the world loving their lives. Yet they're likely to have experienced as much 'pain' as anyone: in fact, they've probably experienced more pain, given they were more likely to have been skiing down that black slope in the blizzard.

And this is – I think – what happens. Our fear quotient is dependent not on how much pain we encounter – but how we *respond* to pain. Let's go back right to the beginning. To our birth. Just to reinforce the idea that life means pain and pleasure, our birth is painful (and pleasurable). Our first experience of the world outside the womb is of pain. It's hard to get our first breath. There's no liquid like we're used to. It's probably very light. And, most likely, not as warm as we'd like.

But it's not the pain of the birth itself that will leave us the lasting impression, but the *environment* in which it is felt. The same level of actual pain will have a different effect depending on how people in the room respond to it. If you're born into a room full of fearful, panicky people, it's going to be a very different effect from being born into a room of calm, loving people.

This is the way we're taught early in our lives about how to interpret pain.

When we experience pain, the way the people around us respond to it then teaches us to respond in a similar way. If we're sick as a child and those around us feel anxious and afraid, then we learn that that's the way to respond to such pain. If we cut or burn ourselves as a child and an adult makes a massive deal about it, then we learn that this is the way to respond to such pain.

This is how many of us 'learn' to respond to pain in whatever form. This is our inheritance. Our parents were probably 'taught' their response to pain by their parents, and so they pass it straight to us.

It comes down to this: we learned either that it was okay and safe to be in pain. Or that it wasn't.

It's safe to be in pain

Most of us were taught that it is neither okay nor safe to be in pain. And this is what generates the growing sackful of fear that we live with and through.

So it's time to start looking at how you are around pain. You'll probably see that you panic a little (or a lot) around any pain. Whether it's cutting your finger or getting the flu, being told something you didn't want to hear or getting bad news over the phone, you'll probably notice that you panic.

So the first thing to tell yourself is that there's nothing to panic about. I've played the game of affirmations before, and they can be very powerful. This was one of my favourites: 'I am safe, no matter what I'm feeling.'

It's beautiful. Because it's a self-cancelling affirmation. You're clearly not feeling safe, but you tell yourself that you are, even if you're feeling that you're not.

> **'I AM SAFE, NO MATTER WHAT I'M FEELING.'**

It's worth trying.

Given that our response to pain is the heart of our own fear, this chapter could more aptly be called Say F**k It to Pain. Because as soon as you crack pain, you'll crack fear.

So start saying F**k It to pain. When you respond to pain, you're only acting out a conditioned response. And all conditioned responses are reversible. When you encounter any pain, counter your immediate response by just saying F**k It.

You are safe. In the end, nothing matters. Give in to pain and you can give in to life.

And as you start to say F**k It to pain, you'll notice a couple of things. Your fear for things will begin to evaporate. And this fear will be replaced by libido: the love and lust for life.

This process has real momentum: the less you fear, the more you crave doing things that would have previously scared you. And the more that you do, the more that you get out there, the more you realize you can do and the more you realize there is to do.

Before long you'll be playing the guitar in Leicester Square, going white-water rafting in Canada, dumping your job and writing a film, or simply telling Hunky Hugh in accounts that you think he's really hunky and would he like to go to see a film (that you've written).

SAY FK IT TO PAIN AND YOU'LL BE SAYING F**K IT TO FEAR.**

So, say F**k It to Pain and you'll be saying F**k It to Fear.

Say F**k It to Food

Food is a problem in the developed world. (And, of course, lack of food is a bigger problem in the developing world, but…) If we're not battling with weight issues, we're struggling to eat the right things: with myriad intolerances and allergies, and with different advice coming from every direction.

In recent years, supermarkets have developed whole ranges of foods that don't seem to contain what you think they should, and this is what we've ended up eating:

★ Wheat-free pasta

★ Cocoa-free chocolate

★ Caffeine-free coffee

★ Sugar-free sweeteners

★ Flour-free bread

★ Dairy-free ice cream

★ Sugar-free cakes

★ Fat-free biscuits

★ Meat-free sausages and burgers

It's just so funny. I'm looking forward to the following prefix: FOOD-FREE. I can't wait to try food-free lasagne, food-free pizza, food-free tiramisu. It'll go down a storm. Just as all the gluten-free and sugar-free stuff is for people who have been told they shouldn't eat these things but can't bear to go without the foods they were eating, so food-free lines will be designed for people who are fasting, or wanting to eat less, but need to go through the process of buying food from the supermarket, opening a packet and throwing things away.

Food-free lasagne is my favourite. It contains a microwavable container inside. You prick the plastic lid with a fork, then pop it in the microwave for just a minute. And it's done. You tear off the lid and inside are just the scraped remains of lasagne. You pop it straight in the bin. And you really feel as if you've gone through the whole meal experience.

That's the problem with fasting, you see. As well as being hungry enough to kill your fellow passengers on the Underground and eat them, you miss the whole thing around meals. So much spare time is created when you stop eating for a bit. And we don't know what to do with it. It's just time that you spend thinking about the food that you're not eating. So smear a plate with ketchup and do the washing up… you'll find your fast goes a whole lot better.

So why all the humour? Because our stuff around food just consumes us. And I find this very funny. In one way or another we spend so long thinking about it.

If we're thinking about sex every 10 seconds, I reckon we're thinking about food for at least seven of the other seconds. It's just amazing how any work gets done in this place.

And I'm being funny about it because that's the first step in the F**k It direction.

Our obsession with food is just crazy. And it's hilarious.

Food (like love and sex) is a major area of meaning for us. Though most of us are probably in denial about that. If we were asked to list the things that really matter to us, we probably wouldn't include food. But it's usually one of the things that matter most.

First, then, it's worth getting conscious around food. Start to notice how much you think about it. Notice what goes on when you think about food. Notice how you are when you're eating.

OUR OBSESSION WITH FOOD IS JUST CRAZY.

Notice how you feel when you eat good food that you think you should be eating. And notice how you feel when you're eating bad food that you think you shouldn't be eating. Notice how you are when you see other people eating either extremely good food or extremely bad food. Notice how you feel when I keep asking you to notice how you feel. Anyway, just start to get an idea of how much food really matters to you.

Next, have a little inward giggle about how you are around food. Otherwise you'll cry.

Food matters so much to us for many reasons.

First, it's the great comforter. If you're uncomfortable about anything, then there's nothing more comforting than a bar of chocolate or a biscuit or some cake. And many of us nowadays spend a lot of time feeling uncomfortable but not wanting to face those feelings.

As well as giving you a surge of energy and feelings of happiness (the serotonin released when we eat chocolate, for example), food fills you up. We fill so we can't fill any more. We fill till we feel ill. We fill because the more we fill, the less we feel. And if we're feeling bad, then feeling is the last thing we want to do. We stuff ourselves until we go numb. There is – in many ways – no room for anything else.

Second, it has an effect on our health. Many conditions and diseases are caused by or heavily influenced by the foods we eat. So it's no wonder that we try to eat this or that 'good' food, and try to cut out other foods. If you're ill and think your diet's got something to do with it, you could end up in the gluten-free, sugar-free, dairy-free, salt-free, meat-free and most certainly humour-free corner of the room.

Third, it has an effect on our body shape. Unlike the apparently positive and immediate effect of food as comforter, the negative effect of pounds being put on is a delayed one. You can stuff yourself silly for weeks and the effect on your body is relatively gradual. But the effect is certain. If you eat too much, you'll put on weight. And we live in fear of this. And when we do get overweight we then live with the constant attempts to eat less. And in the battle with food, the time element always gets you: when you're pigging out, the pleasure is instant but the pain is delayed. And when you're trying to eat less, the pain is instant, but the pleasure delayed.

The thing is, the tension created by worrying about food is as unhealthy for you as any bad food you might eat. So you need to find a way to relax around food.

Once you feel you understand more about what you're like about food, it's a good time to start mumbling F**k It a lot around food.

F**k It is about accepting things just as they are. So what would it feel like to start accepting how you are around food? The battle tends to be around eating the wrong things, or too much, and then feeling terrible about it. So when you next pig out, have a go at not beating yourself up about it. Say, 'F**k It, I always do this, no matter how hard I try, so I might as well accept this part of me.'

Even at the moment of choice. The moment when you're feeling down and you're going through the battle of whether to break your diet and the promises to yourself... just take the

FK IT IS ABOUT ACCEPTING THINGS JUST AS THEY ARE.**

pressure off yourself. Say F**k It and either eat it and accept that or don't eat it and just get on with life. But don't make it such a big thing.

Stop making food such a big thing. If you've lost your job and your girlfriend's dumped you, then have a frickin' chocolate bar. In fact, if you're in the UK, get a cab down to the Mars factory in Slough and do the tour where you can scoop up fistfuls of Maltesers and stuff them into your mouth, or put away whole Mars Bars that haven't even had time to cool.

You'll feel better. And feeling better is good.

F**k It, and stop making food such a big thing.

And that probably means being careful when it comes to diets.

Say F**k It to diets

All diet books are useless and they're laying the world's forests to waste. So pop all your diet books in the recycling bin and plant a tree. In fact, plant a fruit tree, then eat the fruit. You'll lose weight and do the world a favour.

The thing is, it's the tension around diets that's a root of the problem.

So, first of all, accept things as they are: maybe you're a little chubby, maybe you're a complete porker, but accept yourself as you are. At least for a few minutes... then go back to the self-loathing until you can build up the accepting bit to more minutes. But have a go.

Accept your eating habits as they are. You know that eating for you is just a merry-go-round. It seems you have no control in the end. And after a patch of eating less, you lose it and eat a whole shelf-full of biscuits (and we're talking the shelf of a supermarket, not a shelf in your kitchen cupboard).

It's also worth accepting that – to one degree or another, and like every other human being walking this Earth – you're fucked up. You have emotional problems, anxiety, neuroses, fears, low self-confidence... Whatever it is, you ain't too happy with yourself and life, and you're eating to feel better.

Most of us do it. Most of us won't admit it. But look at that word – most – you're not alone in this. So you're fucked up... yes, you're human.

All this acceptance will have the definite effect of relaxing you.

Say F**k It to your diet. And F**k It when the voices start coming up. How about saying F**k It and eating what you really fancy for your next meal? Say F**k It afterwards when you start to feel bad. And go with it and see what happens. If you put on a bit of weight, say F**k It.

My bet is that you'll start to get over your issues around food.

My bet is that once you can eat what the hell you want, you won't need to stuff the whole of a birthday cake into your mouth in one go because you know you can have more later or tomorrow if you want.

My bet is that without so much tension around 'good' and 'bad' foods, you may well start to want to eat some of the foods that you thought were 'good' but were so painful to eat. You'll find that you actually like eating these foods. But don't start thinking they're 'good', just eat what you want and see what happens.

And my bet is that, eventually, you'll start to lose weight. If you're still saying F**k It, you shouldn't really care too much. If it matters less to you that you're putting on weight, then it should matter less to you that you're losing it. Sure, treat yourself to a little smile as you see the scales beneath your feet… but you can still say F**k It and have a choccie bar to celebrate.

WHEN YOU LOSE YOUR DESIRE FOR SOMETHING, THAT'S WHEN YOU START TO GET IT.

So F**k your diet and start saying F**k It. Accept how things are, and how you are, because everything is okay as it is – let food and your body shape matter less to you. And observe what all these zen dudes have been monking on about for so long: that when you lose your desire for something, that's the moment when you start to get it.

Say F**k It in Your Relationships

And thus we enter the minefield. This is maybe the most difficult area of your life to understand how saying F**k It in any way can do anything but fuck up your relationships. Let's see why.

Relationships are like the Times Square of your meaning city.

They are indeed. Relationships are where it all happens, where all the action is, where a lot of your attention is focused and where collisions often occur. The other areas of your meaning city are more predictable: your job is more predictable, as are your friends (generally), as is your health, etc., etc.

RELATIONSHIPS ARE LIKE THE TIMES SQUARE OF YOUR MEANING CITY.

But with relationships, what matters *really* matters. The meaning of it all affects us to our very core. A relationship is about us... and the most intimate way we deal with the outside world. The stakes are higher. And everything is invested:

★ If something hurtful is said, we feel it deeply.

★ If we don't feel heard, we feel like children.

★ If we think we love them more than they do us, we feel pain.

★ If we think they love us more than we love them, we feel guilt.

★ If we get excitement from someone outside the relationship, we feel confused.

★ If they get excitement from outside the relationship, we feel jealous.

If life as we live it is about the relationship between us and the outside world, then your relationship with a partner is the finest thread of that relationship.

In a relationship, we're deeply attached to success, and immensely pained by failure. Because everything in a relationship matters so much, the potential for pain is enormous. And many of us do live out the fairly constant pain of our relationship(s).

In relationships, your meaning environment can change rapidly. This is commonly known as falling in love. When you fall in love, other things matter less. Sometimes the only thing that matters is that person. All your normal perceptions of the world go out of the window. Any rationality that you apply to your life can evaporate.

So people who fall in love commonly do the following: leave families they previously adored, give up jobs and positions, lose friends, change their beliefs, lose their dress sense, lose any sense, start listening to music they previously thought was naff.

Love does funny things to people. Zillions of songs have been written about just this effect. Romantic love, then, is apparently a key challenge to the F**k It way of living, as love seems often to be about the meaning of someone else to you and the subsequent attachment and dependency. We think that these qualities are part and parcel of loving someone.

Saying F**k It can have some surprising effects. The problem is that it's very hard to see what F**k It can do in a relationship. How could any good possibly come of your partner feeling less attached to you or feeling less like you're the centre of their world? We love all that dependency and attachment stuff in relationships. But it does also bring a very obvious and large potential for pain.

SAYING FK IT CAN HAVE SOME SURPRISING EFFECTS.**

And from your position in a loving attachment to someone, it's very difficult to see how feeling less attachment towards them could improve things. But let's have a go.

Think of a relationship where you were deeply in love with someone: smitten by them (and this may well be your present relationship, of course). Remember what it felt like to be attached to them: loving their attention and looks… waiting for their calls… cherishing time with them above everything else. And remember the flip side, too: getting anxious, wondering whether they loved you as much as you loved them… getting jealous easily… getting frustrated with yourself for being so dependent on someone.

Now imagine what it would have been like to have taken things a little less seriously. Imagine if you'd not taken things so personally. Imagine if you hadn't worried about whether it would last forever. Imagine hanging on less to the relationship and letting the other person breathe. Imagine them mattering a tad less to you. Imagine that 'you' weren't at stake in the relationship.

And here's the strange thing: it doesn't mean that you love this person any less.

In fact, this may be where definitions of love start to strain at the leash. Because the clingy, attaching romantic love that we and everything in our society supports as 'love' can transform into another kind of 'love' when we stop clinging.

It's an unexpected outcome, but when there is a tad less meaning, the love seems to increase.

Part of the reason for this, of course, is due to tension and relaxation. When you're attached and dependent, there's an enormous tension in the relationship. There's no room for anything to move.

As soon as something shifts, things start to snap, like a very tight spring just snapping.

When you relax everything – when you relax out of your attachment and investment in the relationship – there's more space and room. And just as *chi* flows more readily in a relaxed body, the love flows more readily in a relaxed relationship.

Whatever your issues and tightness in your relationship, see what it's like to say F**k It to them. Just speak out your issue now. Then say F**k It and see how it feels.

LOVE FLOWS MORE READILY IN A RELAXED RELATIONSHIP.

'I don't feel she finds me attractive like she used to… Well, F**k It.'

And so on.

Whatever stage of your relationship you're in, poke your head out for a mo and see what it's like when you feel that things don't quite matter as much. Feel the relaxation. Feel the freedom. Then carry on with your life and see what happens.

Like the energy that flows through a newly relaxed body, love and energy might start to flow more through you and your relationship.

Or, perhaps, as you release some of the clinginess to the relationship, you might both realize that, F**k It, it's time to move on.

In the end, whether the love moves more in our current relationship or you both move out of that relationship, movement happens. And F**k It does tend to bring movement (from stuckness).

Say F**k It to Money

In our world of meaning, money means a lot. This is of course not true for everyone, but generally:

★ If we don't have much, we wish we had some and that all our money worries would go away.

★ If we have a moderate amount of money, enough not to worry about bills and paying for holidays, we dream of having more, being able to drive a better car or live in a bigger house.

★ If we are wealthy, we still tend to want more, to be financially independent, or to have a holiday home in a foreign land.

★ If we are stinking rich, we tend to worry that we could lose it in the next crash.

If we're not rich, we tend to resent those who are. We judge those who flash money around; we think that 'money can't make you happy'; we know that 'they can't take it with them', and we think it's 'indecent'.

If we're rich, we can be quite defensive about our money: it may be important to us that we 'worked hard for it', or that we're not really *that* rich (not compared to really rich people), and we might deliberately not 'flash it around' by buying a moderate car and not a flashy one.

So, whether you're broke or loaded, money brings its issues. You probably have your issues and judgements around money. You may think that it's okay to be 'comfortably off' but that having too much is immoral.

Well, F**k It. How about having no judgement around money, and accepting things just as they are?

Money is just an abstract means of exchange, after all. It's the messenger in the exchange deal between you and the world. And you know what they say about the messenger: don't shoot them.

This is simply about exchange. If what you have to offer is worth enough to other people, then they'll give you lots of things in return. So, for a moment, imagine that there wasn't any money. If enough of you read this book you'll

HAVE NO JUDGEMENT AROUND MONEY AND JUST ACCEPT THINGS AS THEY ARE.

all offer me something for it. I'm in particular need of flowers for the garden at the moment. So you all give me some flowers. The more of you who read this, the more flowers I'll receive.

By next summer, my garden should be full of flowers and looking beautiful. And that's all being rich is. I offer something you like and you give me something in return for it. I'm happy that I've given you something of value. And I'm happy that my previously barren garden is now full of flowers. That's beautiful: there's nothing dirty or immoral about that, is there?

See the same for what you do. When you work (or whatever you normally do for money), imagine that you're simply offering something of value to the world, and the world values this and gives you something for it. The world values what you do by paying your bills, buying your clothes, taking you out for dinner, sending you on holiday, and turning up at your house with a new car.

You are simply in a constant process of exchange for value with the world.

The more the world values what you do and what you're giving, the more it will give back. Of course, there are times when what the world tends to value is out of step with what we have to offer. As I write this, the world is really appreciating those who have the skill to drive a lorry (because there aren't enough people who can). But in ten years' time, the world probably won't value this skill as highly (because the lorries will probably drive themselves).

Whichever way, what tends to happen is that the more you value yourself, the more the rest of the world will tend to agree and value you as well.

So start by valuing yourself. Listen to the corporate guru L'Oréal: Because You're Worth It.

THE MORE YOU VALUE YOURSELF, THE MORE THE WORLD WILL VALUE YOU.

Enjoy the process of exchange, whether big or small. If you're happy to be humble and self-contained, enjoy the small things that the world brings you for the things that you offer.

If you want to go out and really offer something amazing to the world, lap up the attention and value what you're given in return. Don't be resentful of those who are being given a lot for what they're offering to the world. Enjoy it: enjoy that the world is generous enough to give to those it values.

And don't put any limits on what you think the world should give you. If people continue to read this book, and keep on giving me flowers, I'll continue to accept those flowers and fill my garden with them. One problem I might run into is not having enough water to keep them all alive. So at some point I'll have to stipulate that, while I'd still love to receive flowers, I'd prefer ones that don't need much water. Yes, I could set up a special cactus garden.

And when that's full, I'll truly know I'm officially Stinking Rich.

Say F**k It to some of your money issues, then, by picturing money as simply your exchange relationship with the world. But also say F**k It to money full stop. Money doesn't matter that much, really. A lot of our tension around money is the fear of having none.

So it's a good idea to imagine what it would be like to have none, so you can face that fear head-on. Imagine if you lost all the money and possessions that you have. What would you do? In a society like ours, I'd have thought that most of you could imagine how you'd be able to cope.

If you lost everything, you wouldn't die.

So lose your fear of losing your money. The world will still value what you have to offer, and it will lavish you with gifts once more.

Any attachment around money is, of course, tension. Attachment to getting more, or attachment to keeping what you have – it's all tension.

Saying F**k It to money releases that tension and leaves just softness and relaxation. And, as we're seeing in other areas, when there's relaxation things flow. It's the same with the value exchange we call money. When we relax our hold on money, things tend to flow more naturally. That means that things tend to flow naturally in both directions. If you stop being so uptight about losing money, then you may well start to spend more, invest more and be more generous. And this gets the flow going. You'll tend to find that more money then starts to come your way.

LOSE YOUR FEAR OF LOSING YOUR MONEY.

Money. If you have none, say F**k It and enjoy life as it is. If you have some, say F**k It and start enjoying people valuing you. If you have oodles, say F**k It and start basking in the fruits of the world thinking you're such an amazing person that it throws so much at you.

Say F**k It to Your Job

So, before we get into how shitty working is, let's spend a moment remembering how lucky most of us are today with work.

I can feel the word 'unprecedented' coming up, are you ready? Yes, we live in an age of 'unprecedented' freedom in the workplace. Of course, this doesn't apply to everyone, everywhere, but many of us in the West are experiencing very new freedoms in the workplace.

Generally speaking, if you've got the talent and the determination, you can do well in just about whatever you fancy turning your hand to.

Look at how my family has changed, for example. I'll cross family lines as I pick randomly at these examples, but... my great-grandparents were the cook and gardener of a *Downton Abbey*-like mansion in the Midlands. My grandparents were working in textile factories, often nights, for the whole of their working lives. My father was offered a choice of two careers by his father: 'You can either work for the gas board or in an accountant's office, lad.' He chose accountancy.

None of them sat there with a careers 'counsellor' working out how to match their strengths and abilities with a job role. They didn't go to university 'milk-rounds' where they could suck on the teats of 100 corporates. I was perhaps the first in my family to actually sit there and be able to ask, 'What would I really like to do?' The answer was something creative, so that's what I was able to do.

Of course, things can still be difficult. The 'gig economy' dresses up often low-paid work (with none of the security of an employed position) in the clothes of freedom.

But even for those who do have the freedom and opportunity to choose their line of work, and be paid well for it, most are still not happy. Many of us don't like the work we do or the company we're working for. Work is what we spend most of our time doing, yet many of us are fundamentally unhappy with what we get up to between the hours of 9 a.m. and 7 p.m. There's always trouble at the mill.

MANY OF US ARE FUNDAMENTALLY UNHAPPY WITH OUR WORK.

The first reason is that there's usually too much expectation. The workplace is as littered with unrealistic expectations as it is with crass clichés. Just think about the expectations that surround you and the job that you do: from parents, from friends, from society, from your employer, from your staff, from shareholders, from the government. We do what we do because we think it should be fulfilling us, that there's the possibility of attaining all those material needs (and aims) we have. We expect a lot of a job. Your workplace is now probably also the most important community you belong to.

So your job has a lot to hold in terms of expectation. And the problem is that many of these may be competing with each other: your parents want something to be able to brag about at dinner parties; your partner wants a fat pay cheque; your boss wants long hours and high productivity; you want to spend more time sitting in parks reading.

It's time to unpick the expectations.

Work out what other people are expecting of you (and whether it really matters to you); work out what you are expecting of yourself (and whether that really matters to you). Start to say F**k It to the things that you find actually don't matter so much. Concentrate on the few things that do matter to you and make you feel good. I saw a great comedian last week in London: he was a trained GP (not, I suspect, and hope, that there are that many untrained GPs), had said F**k It and started doing stand-up comedy.

And we've had so many participants of our retreats and workshops who've said F**k It and gone on to switch their line of work: the banker who became a chef, the chef who went travelling, living off a blog, the blogger who became a teacher, the band member who set up a music school, the coach who became a landscape gardener, to mention just a few.

Given we're talking about business, I'll employ my own cliché again: you can't please all of the people all of the time. So don't try.

Start trying to please yourself more and see what happens.

Which brings us to the second reason: too little expectation. If you can relax enough to really feel what you fancy doing, and what you really can't bear doing, then it's worth setting up some expectations about sorting yourself out. If you can't bear the job you're in, expect that you're going to find something better within a month. Expecting positive change (especially when you know specifically what that change should be) works.

And don't get into too much stress about making decisions, moving on, etc. When you really know what you want (through relaxing), it's very difficult for change not to happen quite naturally. It may be that the day after you've realized you'd be mad to carry on working where you are, you get a call from someone who knows of a job elsewhere. Once you're free from the expectations of you, just start to rest in your own expectations for yourself.

Saying F**k It in the context of work isn't just about giving up your job, though. It could be that as you relax you realize you're actually content with the work you do. You may find that simply accepting what you have is the best way to say F**k It. You may find that any unhappiness you feel is from others' (or your own) unrealistic expectations of yourself. Are you going for the director's job because you want it or because you think that's what you should be doing? Do you really need to jump to the next level up and work harder, or could you make do with what you have and maybe even work less?

In my experience, one of the most common statements people make about work is: 'Well, I don't really know what I want to do yet.' I hear this from people in their 30s and 40s, not just those in their 20s. People go on saying this for years and years. And this is the only articulation they have for a deep sense of things not being right. They've chosen their work area to articulate this unease, but the reasons for the unease are probably more complex. What they're really saying is, 'I don't know myself, but I get the feeling there's something wrong in there.'

If this is speaking to you, it's time to stop hiding behind the words 'I don't really know what I want to do yet.' Say F**k It and find the courage to get to know yourself. What do you really want of yourself and for yourself? Find somebody who can help you work it through if you fancy, but the chances are it's not just about your job, it's about your life. And I guess the problem for you is what most of us face: that we have many competing (usually unknown) forces at work in us.

I've observed this phenomenon in recent years: that everybody wants to be 'everything'. There's so much pressure on people to be everything that it's irresistible. We all want to be successful at work, experts in the home (at cooking, gardening, DIY), hard-working employees, present and available partners and parents, home-owners and wealthy.

SAY FK IT AND FIND THE COURAGE TO GET TO KNOW YOURSELF.**

We all want to live sustainable lifestyles, be on-the-ball mentally and culturally, feel relaxed and peaceful, see the world, but not fly too often. Everything's speeding up in a performance culture. Even in yoga classes, people are looking around wondering how quickly they'll be able to do that difficult-looking *asana*, or whether the *pranayama* exercise can bring peace to every area of their life.

I feel tense just writing about it.

Of course, sifting through your own desires is difficult. You'd like to be financially secure – with a home abroad – but also to work less in a less stressful job. Some desires can sit next to each other, while some compete. Start working it out.

Me? I don't usually do any work. I just do things I like. And I've stopped liking writing about work, so it's time to move on.

Say F**k It to Your Country

> ME? I DON'T USUALLY DO ANY WORK. I JUST DO THINGS I LIKE.

*When I originally wrote this chapter, in 2005, we had, a couple of years before, said F**k It to the UK, and moved to Italy. We recently moved back to the UK (after 15 years), just before 'Brexit' happened. Sadly, it is now much more difficult for a British person to hop over to a European country, as we and many others did, or for a European person to hop over to Britain, as many also did. I'm hoping you live in a country where it is relatively easy to move somewhere else if you so fancy, otherwise you'll end up reading this section and feeling sad too.*

I swapped countries. I now live in a warmer, more relaxed, more laid-back, happier, less competitive country (Italy), and I'm happy with that. When I go back to the UK I find it – in about equal measures – inspiring, motivating, alive, buzzing… but also overcrowded, over-competitive, striving, messy, uptight and neurotic.

It's another expression of modern freedom that many of us do have the ability to move country without having been forced out of our own (through war, starvation, etc.).

If you've had enough, and you want more sun, why not? Say F**k It and get on a plane (or, more responsibly, on a train – or, even more responsibly, walk it). But here's something to remember first: we take ourselves with us wherever we go.

This is, of course, obvious. In a very literal way, we can't help but take ourselves with us. We don't have a 'to do' list saying 'passport, tickets, skeleton, internal organs, musculature and all the bits in between'. But we do tend to take with us all the problems that we assume were caused by things around us. If you think you're unhappy because of the rain, the people, your job, the uptight men – whatever it is you think you're running away from – have another think.

Because the chances are that all the unhappiness is within you.

And wherever you go – whatever paradise you find – all that unhappiness will come bubbling back up again sooner or later.

Now, of course, it may take giving it all up and living somewhere else to really realize this. Even though I'm telling you this right now, you probably don't believe it – in which case it's best to get on with it so you can prove to yourself that this is the truth, and then get on with your life.

HERE'S SOMETHING TO REMEMBER: WE TAKE OURSELVES WITH US WHEREVER WE GO.

I do know this through experience. I helped three burly men pack a lorry up with our stuff. I thought I was keeping my eye on the stuff: making sure they didn't break anything precious, or leave bits behind that we wanted, or pick up things that we didn't want. But somehow, somewhere in that lorry were hidden all my issues, anxieties, anger, annoying habits and irrational mood swings.

So, I'm here now, sitting in what you'd probably think of as a paradise, with a lot of the same shit going on. Though for me, the very process of realizing that I am all that stuff wherever I go has been very liberating. And I may not have got to that liberation if I'd stayed sitting at that desk in London.

Relax, let go, and then see if you really need to move. If you prefer to stay, then accept your life and your country for what it is.

Hey, modern me back again. So you're wondering why we moved back to the UK aren't you? Here's something: it's really hard to know where will suit you the most. The world is full of people in cities longing to live near the sea or in the countryside, people in the countryside desperate for the buzz and life of the city. The pandemic has seen lots of Londoners running for the hills. But I guess that lots of them will be running back before long. We've tried the big city, the isolated farmhouse on a hill in a hot country, the small town at the seaside in a hot country, and we're back now mixing it all up by living in a small city by the seaside (Brighton-Hove, UK). We'll see.

Say F**k It Around Parenting

If you have kids, this section will work for you, as it's a reminder of the lessons we can learn from our kids that make all the difficult bits worth it.

If you don't have kids, I'd suggest you still stick around, because I roll into talking about how kids are a great metaphor for life itself. And you wouldn't want to miss that, would you? In fact, I'd go as far as to say that spending just a few minutes reading about the nature of parenting, and then learning about the blessed gift that parents receive from their kids, rather than going through years of parenting in order to receive that gift, is a very efficient use of your time.

Becoming a parent is a big thing. I can see the whole process was designed to ease you into the idea of having children around. After all, you get nine months – nine whole months, that's practically a year of your life – to start getting used to the idea.

But nothing – not even these nine months – can prepare you for what it's like to have children. We have non-identical twin boys, Arco and Leone, born in August 2001. At 4 a.m. on the night after they were born, I got up for the hundredth time to change one of them – which was a weird experience in itself because no one had ever told me they wouldn't be shitting, well, shit, for a while, but rather they'd be shitting melted chocolate. So there I was in the anaemic early morning light, getting accustomed to a new routine of wiping shit from my baby's body and re-applying the plastic safety nets ready for the next expulsion.

And I looked around and thought, No, this is okay. I can do this. Yes, I feel tired. But I can do it. I can get through it.

But then I realized that I didn't have to get through just this one night. That it wasn't like working through the night on a last-minute college essay, handing it in just before the 10 a.m. deadline and then going to sleep for a few days. No, siree. This certainly wasn't just tonight. This was tonight and tomorrow night and the night after and the night after that and on and on and on.

And I groaned.

But then one of my new baby boys chuckled. And I melted.

And over the next few weeks I learned that everything is designed to be in perfect balance. The utter hell of the first few weeks, mainly caused by severe sleep-deprivation, was perfectly balanced by the absolute heaven of having two such incredible beings suddenly appearing as the most important thing in my life.

Parenthood is nothing short of astonishing. It's impossible to describe the love you feel for your own children. It goes beyond anything I've ever experienced before. Your children constantly remind you what it's all about. And I know that's a cliché, which we'll examine in a minute, but it's true.

At the time I was writing the original edition of this book, our boys, who were still very young, mostly spoke Italian. But then one of them started speaking to me in English. He said everything in English, and it was a miracle. My heart melted every time he said anything. A typical conversation:

YOUR CHILDREN CONSTANTLY REMIND YOU WHAT IT'S ALL ABOUT.

'Daddy, what you doing, Daddy?'

'I'm writing a book.'

'A book, Daddy? Where is it?'

'It's in here, inside here.'

'Inside the computer, Daddy?'

'Yes, and one day it will be a real book.'

'Can I see it, Daddy?'

'Yes, this is it, here.'

'Where, Daddy?'

'Inside here…'

So I suddenly had a gift that most parents don't have: one of my children speaking my own language proficiently, all of a sudden. No 'cat', 'dog', 'daddy', 'mummy'… but 'Me been to the sea, Daddy, and play in tree, Daddy.' It was just amazing.

My boys mean a lot to me. With Gaia, they mean everything to me.

So here we are, in a book about saying F**k It, talking about meaning causing pain and how things don't really matter as much as you think… and we bump up against the major irrefutable meaning of the children in our lives.

So let's get one thing straight: meaning is not wrong. Some things will always have meaning for you and for me. There's no need to feel bad that your children mean more than the world to you.

But children do give you an insight into your world of meaning. It's not possible to anticipate what it'll be like to have children because it's impossible to see how much your world of meaning can change.

Just weeks after having your first child or children, you can't imagine what it was like not to have children. You can't imagine what you did with your time. You can't imagine why you used to worry about the things you used to worry about.

Having children is a major Perspective Machine. The things that mattered to you before, that had meaning for you, tend to humbly drop to their knees and start to shuffle apologetically out of the door, recognizing the awesome superior meaningfulness of the new arrivals.

Everything changes. And it demonstrates to us that meanings are not fixed. That they shift and change. Within one month of our boys being born, I said F**k It to a career that was previously important to me. It meant nothing any more. And I went with that.

So parenthood brings with it a natural level of F**k It. We naturally think F**k It to some of the things that previously mattered to us. Folks previously lost in how they looked and what they wore are seen out at the local café in baggy jumpers with sick on their shoulders. Captains of industry with reputations for not suffering fools gladly are seen in sunny parks entertaining chuckling infants with coochycoochycoo noises and making peculiar faces and looking like, well, yes, like fools.

Being a parent gives you a unique insight into what it's like to say F**k It to lots of things in your life.

PARENTHOOD BRINGS WITH IT A NATURAL LEVEL OF FK IT.**

But what about parenting itself?

The first phenomenon of parenting is that everything is new and difficult. Looking after children is a very difficult job. And you don't get to go to college to learn the skills. You don't even get to go to evening classes. All you get is ante-natal classes (Why don't they change the name for a start? This can confuse people: 'Why should I go to classes run by people who are 'anti-natal'? I want to talk to people who are 'pro-natal', for Christ's sake.' It's not a good start, is it?).

These classes, though, only cover the pregnancy and birth. The best you get is a crash course in how to cope with the first day: i.e. changing nappies and how to hold your baby.

It's a bit like astronauts going to ante-take-off evening classes, and being taught everything about preparing for the take-off: 'Now, remember, the take-off could be difficult for all of you, you've got to help each other, look after one another. And don't forget to have your take-off bag ready just in case. Make sure you have your pyjamas, some spare underwear and your anti-gravitational-sickness tablets. The main thing is to enjoy it. Take-off is a beautiful process and one you'll remember for the rest of your lives.'

Which is all very well and good, but what happens once they're up in space?

'Houston, can you read me? This is Apollo 21; repeat, Apollo 21.'

'Coming through loud and clear, Apollo 21. That was some take-off. We're all totally pissed on all that champagne down here, and are hugging, Apollo 21.'

'Read you, Houston. But, Houston…'

'Yes, Apollo 21…?'

'What do we do now?'

'Errmm, what do you mean, Apollo 21?'

'Well, there's, like, loads of, like, dials and switches and stuff, and every time I take my seat belt off I start flying all over the place, and I can't even have a crap without it starting to float around like some frickin' sci-fi movie… What the heck is going on up here, Houston?'

That's what it's like being a new parent. The only preparation you thought you were supposed to do for this post-birth period was to paint the nursery in bright colours and spend a fortune on stuff you don't really want.

After a couple of days of chaos you're on Amazon, looking for help. Fortunately, this has happened before, so someone thoughtful has written a book called *F**k, I'm a Parent, What the Hell Do I Do Now?* and the pages are laminated so you don't ruin the book with piss, sick or liquid shit.

So you read the book and you feel out of your depth and this is what happens: whenever we're unsure about something, a vacuum is created. And unless you live in a scientific laboratory where it's possible to create a vacuum in glass tubes by sucking out the air before sealing them and keeping them that way, then your vacuum is going to try to suck in stuff.

FORTUNATELY, THERE'S A BOOK CALLED *FK, I'M A PARENT, WHAT THE HELL DO I DO NOW?***

And, guess what? The whole world wants to fill your vacuum. Because everyone thinks they know about parenting. And they certainly think they know more than the tired-looking you does.

And you start to get advice from every quarter.

You'll get advice from your parents, other mothers, people in the street, the medical profession, the government, even the Church.

I think giving unsolicited advice to new parents is a form of bullying: you catch someone who's acutely and chronically sleep-deprived, at their most vulnerable, and then bombard them with information.

But that's what vacuums do: they attract stuff that wants to fill them.

So it's a good idea to either seal your vacuum, or at least to put a filter on the gap that's sucking stuff in.

If you seal your vacuum, this is what you have to do: you have to realize that every single parent has gone through this uncertain patch of thinking they know nothing. So it's worth relaxing into this feeling. You then have to recognize that you do indeed know a good deal of the basics: you know how to change your baby, console your baby, feed your baby and dress your baby. And that – for a while at least – is all you need to know.

SAY FK IT AND DO WHAT YOU THINK IS BEST.** The rest, you can make up. Say F**k It to the barrage of advice and ideas about routine and sleeping patterns, and do what you think is best. The advice you'll receive about a whole host of things 'baby' is just the advice that's in fashion at that moment. By next month it'll have changed. And you risk subjecting your dearest to a theory that will soon be replaced by another theory.

The next thing about parenting will surprise you: most parents are scared of their children. Now I don't mean in a Damien out of *The Omen* kind of way. I'm not suggesting that people are wondering whether they've spawned a messenger from the Underworld.

No, this is what I mean: fear derives from experience of – and therefore anticipation of – pain. And there's a lot of pain for parents around their children. There's clearly a lot of fear at the beginning. But we've talked enough about the beginning. Let's look at bringing up children once they've passed the involuntary pooing stage.

So to see why you'll be 'scared' of your children, just look at what they do that causes you pain:

★ They go into wild, stroppy moods.

★ They say 'no' when you ask them to do something.

★ They misbehave in restaurants and other public places.

★ They are always making a racket when you want some peace.

★ They're always wanting you to buy them something new.

So you develop, consciously or unconsciously, some fear around your children.

And this is what we do with that fear: we try to control our children. We impose discipline and 'boundaries' and we let them know that it's okay to do some things and not okay to do others. We force them to sit still in restaurants. We tell them that they have to be quiet when Daddy is reading his newspaper. We shout at them if they're in a mood until they stop being in a mood. And we threaten them when they do anything we don't want them to.

And the whole of society will support a strict disciplinarian approach to parenting. This is because everyone has this fear within them of what children might do.

MOST PARENTS ARE SCARED OF THEIR CHILDREN.

It's as if children are monsters (how many times have you heard parents say, 'Oh, he's a little monster') who can turn round and eat us at any time.

Children are beautiful, innocent and pure beings. Nothing a child does is wrong. The problem is our thinking that what they do is wrong. A child can do no wrong.

So, it's time (for you at least) to say F**k It to this fear. And this is why:

★ The less you try to control your kids, the more they'll take care of themselves.

★ The less you discipline them, the better (generally) they'll behave.

This is a beautiful way to look after children because it's much less effort. If you've tried to teach your child or children how to sit still at the dinner table, you know how difficult 'controlling' children can be. Children are raw life-force. They sometimes want to run around and play and they sometimes want to rest. That's what life does. There is night and there is day. There is rest and there is play. And with a child – like life – if you try to impose 'sitting still' on them when they want to move around, you're in for a struggle.

It's much easier to go with their rhythm than to try and impose yours.

Have a go at doing less rather than more. If you're about to stop your child from doing something or to tell them off, just hold yourself back and ask yourself whether it's worth waiting this time and seeing what happens if you don't.

If you take this course of less effort and intervention, you'll invariably get some shit from other people. You'll get some looks in restaurants and in shops. And it's up to you where you decide that 'It's just their shit' and where they have a point (i.e. it must be darn disturbing here in the Savoy to have children leaping from table to table dressed as Spider-Man).

And if you're thinking, *Yeah, sure, sounds great in theory, but I'm sure it's a nightmare in practice*, listen to this: in the end, as parents, we don't 'know', we only sense.

So don't be scared of your kids, accept every part of them and let them be free.

You can control kids as much as you can control life. In other words, you can't (very easily).

Saying F**k It around parenting is giving in to what kids are. Just as saying F**k It to life is giving in to what life is. And the two things are practically the same. As kids are pure, unadulterated (hey, look at that word: un-adult-erated – cool) life energy. If you get used to saying F**k It to how your kids are, in all their playing, their sulking, their screaming and their tenderness, you'll very quickly learn how to get used to saying F**k It to life.

Say F**k It to Religion

Oh, please, just do. It's probably a good idea to just say F**k It to organized religion and all the nonsense that it involves.

And just to check:

★ If the religion involves you thinking you're right and everyone who doesn't believe the same thing as you is wrong, please get out as quickly as you can.

★ If the religion involves thinking that it is wrong, sinful or evil to do things that are natural and beautiful and life-enhancing –

such as desiring to have sex, having sex, and having sex with members of your own sex – then get out as quickly as you can.

★ If the religion involves denying facts that are patently true, such as the shape of the Earth, the age of the Earth and its inhabitants, and how the inhabitants evolved over millions of years, then get out as quickly as you can.

★ If the religion is drenched in the stink of persecution, racism, sexism, homophobia and paedophilia, don't even go there in the first place.

If you're drawn to exploring the spiritual, keep an open mind and avoid the dogma.

Keep respect, kindness, openness, love and curiosity at the heart of any spiritual exploration you undertake.

And that probably therefore means saying F**k It to organized religion.

Say F**k It to the Weather

I giggle when people complain about the weather.

Every day we are surrounded by things that don't suit us. The sound of the dog barking next door, the way our partner ignores us over breakfast, the traffic jam on the way to work, being handed another project with a tight deadline, being hassled by the office bore…

And we believe that we can exert some control over these things that get us down: we could give the dog a treat to keep it quiet (no, don't lace it with poison), tell our partner to give us some attention, leave for work earlier, say no to the project and tell the office bore to go bore someone else.

A very harmonious way to live with an awkward world would be to try to change what pisses us off, or just accept it as it is.

The difficult way to live is to not do a thing about what pisses us off, and not accept it either... so we spend our days being pissed off about things we're not willing to do anything about. And this is how many of us live.

If this sounds somewhat dysfunctional, then, to me, it seems hilariously dysfunctional to start complaining about the weather. Because this really is one thing we can do nothing about. Usually not today, anyway. In the long term, you can move abroad and buy yourself some different weather, but for now, this is it.

TO COMPLAIN ABOUT THE WEATHER IS THE MOST ABSURD EXAMPLE OF NOT ACCEPTING THE WORLD AS IT IS.

To complain about the weather is the most absurd example of not accepting the world as it is.

So say F**k It to the weather, whatever it is, especially in a country like the UK. Relax into the weather. Look up at the grey skies and think that it's a little like living in a Tupperware container. Enjoy the sound of rain on the car roof. Huddle close to the fire in your local pub when it's cold. And soak up the sun whenever it comes out.

Say F**k It to Getting Older

What was I going to write about saying F**k It and getting older, ooohhh, I had some thoughts but now can't quite remember what they were, ahhh, I'm forgetting things more these days, oh well, F**k It…

… is pretty much what this chapter is about.

Oof, this is not so easy to write, as contemplating the downsides of ageing isn't easy. I'm also aware that a good many of you reading this might not even be thinking about ageing at all. So either make a mental note (in your sharp young brain) that you can come back to this chapter one day in years to come, when you are thinking more about ageing, or enjoy reading what's likely to be in store further down the line.

Let me put off talking about the downsides of ageing, for a moment anyway, by talking about the upsides.

When this book was first published and a friend of my parents – he would have been in his 70s then, I think – asked me what I was up to, and I replied, 'I've just written a book called *F**k It* about sitting back more and taking things less seriously', I braced myself for an uncomfortable silence or difficult exchange (he was a member of the same church as my parents). But he went on to talk lyrically about how F**k It he felt in his later years; how he felt more free and just didn't care so much. I beamed as much as my parents fumed (the whole F**k It thing generally made them quiet or angry).

I was very inspired by him too: I've often thought of that exchange and it's a great reassurance that age might bring even more of a F**k It sense in my life.

And I do get it.

At every adult decade birthday so far (i.e. 30, 40 and 50), I've said something to the effect of 'Oh, I love being [insert age], because it means there's less pressure now.' I said it enthusiastically at 30. I said it emphatically at 40. And I did say it at 50, though it was more out of habit. I had an underlying doubt that time, I knew something was coming.

And what happened in the few years after my 50th birthday was a growing awareness that I might well have a good few years left on this planet (and if you're reading this with the knowledge that I *didn't* get many more good years on this planet after writing this bit – well I look a bit stupid, don't I? Ah well, F**k It, I'm dead, what does it matter?). It felt as though, up to 50, I wasn't really looking far ahead on the road of life. I probably didn't see much past the next decade fork in the road. In my 20s, 30 probably seemed way off and a bit old. The same in my 30s, with 40, and I know I felt that in my 40s because I do remember thinking, when people hit 50, *Oohh, that's a bit old*. But I never really imagined anything beyond these forks. Of course, I did know that people lived beyond these forks. There have always been old people in my life, like there probably are for you. I remember the moment my parents turned 30, after all: FOGIES. So I knew in theory that old age existed.

But it was like knowing that the moon exists: I know it exists but I don't ever imagine what it would be like to visit or live there.

And then, post-50, the whole road suddenly opened up, off into the distance (or a rocket vapour trail up to the moon if you prefer to continue that analogy). *Oh*, I thought, *I might conceivably be here for a few more decades*. Pause. *F**k. What do I do now then?*

And amidst all the thoughts of decrepitude and slow or fast decline and a losing of one's powers (sorry, this is supposed to be the upside bit), I thought *Ooohhh, maybe I'll start to feel even more F**k It, really naturally, as if things really genuinely don't matter so much; GREAT!*

I'll let you know in the next update, in 10 years' time, how it's going on that score. If I'm here. And if I can write. And if I can remember that I was going to update you (note to editor: do you folks have a diary system where you could make a note to message me in 10 years' time and remind me about this please?).

Another upside bit is that, of course, we have the wisdom of our years. Of simply being around for longer. I very rarely spout any wisdom to our now 20-year-old sons. But I do find myself saying things like this: 'Well, having been an adult for 35-plus years now, I can tell you that that kind of thing doesn't happen very often, so I wouldn't worry.'

Right, downsides.

Oh my, I really am resisting this bit.

I keep distracting myself. Once, just now, to get a chunk of cheese. Then again, to have a quick check of the plants in our garden (yeah, I'm in my 50s; I wouldn't have been doing that pre-50, I can tell you).

And maybe this is how I'll age. Constantly distracting myself from it. Pretending it's not happening. Getting caught by surprise when I put my shoulder out, or forget something, or realize that I can't do more than 20 press-ups without aching the next day, or wondering why people are looking at me when I'm dancing on the sea-front to someone else's ghetto-blaster (yes, I deliberately used a term there for an amplification device straight from my youth).

I'm good at pretending age is not really happening.

A few weeks ago, I heard the tune of an ice-cream van for the first time in a long, long time. It thrilled me. It brought back memories. And immediately I was shoes on and out to get a '99' (an ice cream in a cone with a chocolate flake

I'M GOOD AT PRETENDING AGE IS NOT REALLY HAPPENING.

stuck in). After that afternoon, I didn't hear the ice-cream van for a while. When I next heard it, last week, I was, again, shoes on and out, walking the 100 yards to pick up my 99. But halfway there, the ice-cream van set off, tune blaring again. I couldn't believe it. Had he not looked down the pavement to check if there was anyone on their way for an ice cream?

By now, I was rather set on the thought of that 99.

So I started to run. In fact, I went from the pavement onto the road to run, in the hope that he might see me. Now, I'm not a runner, and I'm not the thinnest person on the street (and that's probably part of the problem: the street is full of thin people who don't want to eat frozen sugar and milk in the afternoon).

So what we have now, if you happened to look out of your window that afternoon, is an ice-cream van, tune playing, with a fat old guy chasing it down the road.

Anyway, I nearly caught him. But I didn't. And my legs were burning.

That scene demonstrates my resistance to ageing: in the first place, I shouldn't really have been thinking about 99s and lollies. And in the second place, I certainly shouldn't have been running down the road after that van.

I could sit here and contemplate how I'm going to need to come to terms, over the next however-long-I-have, with the slowing speed, the diminishing powers, the faltering memory and sharpness, the pains and aches and bits that are wearing out or dropping off.

But, for now, I want to say F**k It to Ageing. I want to keep chasing the ice-cream vans, dancing to other people's music on the beach, thinking (as I do sometimes) *I'll sleep when I'm dead*, shouting at people when they refer to my age with any hint of disdain, feeling the excitement today that I felt as an 18-year-old (even if it's for plants rather than parties).

Say F**k It to Fashion

When we say F**k It, we're redressing an imbalance, and usually one that we've previously been unaware of. We start to realize that we've been listening too much to what the world, and others, want of us: we've been too stuck on how we should be or behave.

The movement of F**k It, then, is to listen more to ourselves and our own wisdom: what do *I* want, what do *I* think, how do *I* want to be and behave?

It is thus a movement away from the fashion of the day, one in which we tune in to what our own way is. And this is 'fashion' in the broadest sense: what's currently in and popular in style and the arts and also in behaviour and opinion and even in a political stance.

THE MOVEMENT OF FK IT IS TO LISTEN TO OURSELVES AND OUR OWN WISDOM .**

The F**k It step is to say, 'I won't wear something, or style my hair, or listen to that music, or go to that restaurant, or hold that opinion, or believe that belief because that's what's "in" at the moment;

instead I'll find my own way by listening to myself, not the fashion gurus of style or opinion.'

Taking this F**k It approach to fashion means that sometimes we'll be in step, and sometimes we won't. We reject the path of blindly following fashion, even fashions in thinking. And we take the path of self-awareness and critical thinking: assessing what might be 'right' for us rather than what's 'in'.

Say F**k It and Be Ordinary

It's not fashionable to be ordinary. It hasn't been for a long time.

The jewels of achievement, success, being exceptional in your field, defying the odds, climbing the mountains, being famous (if only in your own backyard), having a following, accumulating letters after your name and punching above your weight are too dazzling for most to resist.

The stories that we are told, and have been told for so long, involve the progression from ordinary to extraordinary via challenges that are overcome.

We have all most likely been heavily influenced by the 'American Dream' and the cultural machine that feeds it: that anyone can do it, with enough work and will; that anyone can battle against the odds to make it to the top and fulfil their God-given gift to be exceptional.

And, also emerging from America, and Silicon Valley in particular, the hungry machine of social media feeds this exceptionalism, as our ability to share with our peers our non-ordinariness is tested moment to moment by 'likes' and 'shares'.

Of course, to follow your heart, to refine your natural gifts, to pursue a talent and share it with the world, is a beautiful thing.

But it's become a zero-sum game: a game in which one person's gain is another's loss (and thus the net gain is zero). In appreciating the exceptional in all its forms, we've learned to diminish and overlook the ordinary. Where the exceptional ones have gained, the ordinary ones have lost.

To fully appreciate the ordinary we have to – for a moment at least – say F**k It to the cult of exceptionalism. We are so deeply embedded in this cult that our perspective is always exceptional-based. Even in our own lives. We tend to recall most easily our successes, our achievements, our high-point moments. We tend not to dwell so much on the vast landscape of time and experience in between the exceptional peaks (or the exceptional troughs for that matter).

TO FULLY APPRECIATE THE ORDINARY, WE HAVE TO SAY FK IT TO THE CULT OF EXCEPTIONALISM.**

Life is made up, even for the most exceptional people, of vast swathes of rather 'ordinary' times and experiences. We humans spend much of our time sleeping, eating, preparing and clearing up around meals, walking, sitting in cars or on trains, chatting with friends, answering emails, cleaning our teeth and washing our bodies, watching unexceptional programmes on unexceptional screens, listening to news today that's generally forgotten tomorrow.

Most of us lead, generally, unexceptional lives, and even the exceptional lives are filled with vast periods of unexceptional moments. Which is kind of a bummer if your view is skewed by being a member of the exceptional cult, and value is given only to the exceptional.

So flip the view for a moment.

Find the value in the ordinary. See the beauty in all the things you do in between the exceptional moments. Revel in the ordinary. And revel in your ordinariness. Enjoy being you at your most ordinary. The exceptional mentality rests on the urge to be unique and different. Sit back for a moment into your ordinariness, your similarity to others in so many ways. Sit back into being one of the crowd, this beautiful crowd of human beings that is sharing this moment of history with you for a while. We don't need to be above anyone else. We don't need to stand out. We can sit back, with a cup of something hot (or chilled, depending on your local climate at this moment), and enjoy the show.

Enjoy the cosiness of sitting back with everyone else and being ordinary.

And 'cosy' is a very berated concept. It's very much looked down on by the exceptional brigade.

Feel the cosiness and relaxation in your body and mind as you embrace your ordinary.

Yes, say F**k It to the rest, to the clamour of exceptionalism, and BE ORDINARY.

Say F**k It to Being a Peaceful Person

For a long time I wanted to be a peaceful and calm person. I remember years ago writing a list of the things I wanted the most.

Top of the list was Peace (just in case you're wondering, next up was an original Chopper bike).

I spent years in my search for peace: practising Chi Kung and meditation every day, trying to work through the issues that made me un-peaceful, getting to know people who seemed to live in peace. I found a good deal of peace through practice, especially Chi Kung. And I imagined that if I could just practise more I'd eventually end up perpetually in the Chi Kung state (this is a light trance state where you're completely relaxed and *chi* is flowing evenly round your body).

I imagined myself as a cool mountain: light activity on the surface, but rock-solid deep down.

I imagined myself as a Taoist monk: gently and calmly carrying out the day's activities in peace and mindfulness. I imagined myself as being like my friend Richard, who remains calm and peaceful no matter what is happening.

I imagined that if only I worked harder at being peaceful, I would eventually make it.

But no matter how hard I tried, no matter how much I practised and how much I looked at my issues, I kept coming up against one big problem on my path to peace: me. Even if I meditated for three hours, I would still return to me in the end.

And this is me: sure, I can be peaceful and calm, generous and kind, centred and balanced. But I can also be stressed and anxious, angry and aggressive, afraid and nervous, selfish and cold.

I recognized, therapeutically, that it was important to let out the 'negative' emotions. And I imagined that if I looked at them enough, and vented them enough (in a healthy environment, of course), they would eventually be vented, and be no more.

Then one day I realized that what I was doing was not that different from what my mother has always done, and I have so heavily judged: as a Christian, she regards her 'good' side as holy and of God, and her 'bad' side as sinful, and sin is of the Devil. I've always had trouble understanding how anyone can look at themselves and their own characteristics and believe that they come from a dark and evil force. When she eats too much she regards it as gluttony, a sin.

For most of us it's a bummer, but for her it's a sin. So she spends her life trying to battle the dark force with her God-inspired light sabre of peace. But the Darth Vader of sin is always there for her, often in the form of oven-baked chicken nuggets or Black Forest gateau.

In response to these perpetual episodes of Christian *Star Wars*, I celebrated the power of the whole human being. I loved being me, in whatever form that took, from an early age.

But then somehow I got into a peace trip.

And, yes, one day I realized that wanting to be peaceful and monk-like was just making me judgemental about all the bits in me that aren't. In my own way I was making relaxation, peacefulness and generosity right and holy. And I was making stress, anger and selfishness wrong and unholy.

So I said F**k It to trying to be anything other than who I am, in this moment. I stopped judging myself. And shit, what a relief that was. What a relief it is.

I SAID Fk IT TO TRYING TO BE ANYTHING OTHER THAN WHO I AM.**

Every emotion I feel is absolutely okay, just as it is.

If I feel love and peace, that's just the same as when I feel fear and anxiety. This is what 'acceptance' and 'non-judgement' really mean. You can't say: 'Okay, I won't get so down about my anger, but of course it's better to be peaceful.' No. They are both the same. That is non-judgement.

And there's a fantastic side effect to accepting yourself for whoever you are: you start accepting other people for who they are, too. It may not happen straight away, but it definitely starts to happen. And it happens for a very simple reason: whenever you judge other people, it simply comes from a non-acceptance of yourself in all your parts.

Jesus himself started to hint at this when he said: 'Love one another as you love yourself.' Now, I know he hadn't had the privilege of training in Gestalt psychoanalytical theory back then, but he did miss out one darn big thing in this: that most people don't love themselves at all. And it's because they don't love themselves that they're so shitty to everyone else.

Sorry, Jesus, but may I suggest that this would have been a better line: 'Love yourselves, dudes, then you'll start loving everyone else and we can all get together in one big, hippie, free-love festival type thing and strip off our sandals and rub each other's beards. Peace and love, dudes.'

Maybe Jesus actually did say this, but stuffy old Matthew, Mark, Luke and John took the good bits out. Judas was probably sitting there smoking a reefer saying, 'Hey, dudes, what about the bit He said about the love fest? That was far out.'

And Matthew just turned round and punched him.

Judas protested: 'Shit, man, it was only a thought.'

And Luke stood up and kicked him hard in the balls.

Judas shut up after that.

Perhaps you too want to be a calm and peaceful person. Perhaps you want to be a kind and generous person. Or perhaps you want to be a ruthless and cold person. Whenever you define the limits of what you want to be, you're going to make the other parts of yourself 'wrong', and that means you're on a hiding to nothing. Even the person who wants to be ruthless and cold is going to feel love and warmth occasionally, and they'll start kicking themselves for having those feelings.

So say F**k It to whatever you want to be. And just be who you are. There's no need to be anything else. There's no need to self-develop, or improve. There's no need to be like anyone else.

You are just fine exactly as you are right now. Just feel that now. All those bits of you that you don't like, that you're embarrassed about, they're all fine. What you think of as your worst side is just the same as what you think of as your best side.

SAY Fk IT TO WHATEVER YOU WANT TO BE, AND JUST BE WHO YOU ARE.**

When you're angry, anxious, jealous, ruthless, that's all the same as when you're calm, peaceful, generous and loving.

Because that's you. And it's me. And everyone else on this planet. And to pretend otherwise would mean we'd have to go off and start a religion with the catchy title: 'I am only this and not that, you know.'

That's all religions are, really. Only they add another line, which always gets me down, so that in total it becomes: 'I am only this and not that, you know. And if you are what I think I'm not, then you're wrong. And you'll burn in hell for it.'

Say F**k It and Be Selfish

We think we have to go to gurus and teachers and priests for wisdom. But every time you fly, one piece of timeless wisdom just passes you by. It occurs during the safety message. I mean, I understand why you're not listening: the brochure full of swanky perfumes and expensive watches is far more interesting than learning how to save your life, isn't it? (No, you're right, though – people just don't survive plane crashes, so you might as well smell nice and have a nice watch to see the time of the moment before you die.)

Okay, this is what you're missing: 'In case of a drop in pressure, oxygen masks will drop down from the panel above you. Please be sure to fit your own oxygen mask before attending to the children in your care.'

Bam. It always causes a bit of a shock when I hear this, even before I had children. Of course, if you think about it, it makes eminent sense to sort yourself out quickly and then focus on your children. After all, you're no good to them dead, which is what you could well be once you've struggled trying to get masks on them while you're unable to breathe yourself. But it's still a bit of a shock to receive an official instruction to look after yourself before anyone else – especially your own children.

The backdrop to our slightly shocked response to this message is the following:

★ It's good to be selfless.

★ It's bad to be selfish.

If you hear on the news that so-and-so carried out a selfless act, then that's something to admire.

If you hear from a girlfriend that so-and-so was just so selfish, then it's never a good thing.

You'd never hear on the news that someone has been lauded for their selfish act. And you'd never hear from your girlfriend that someone was a selfless bastard.

And, like anything that we go through life without questioning, it's worth having a good look at this one – especially if you're interested in following the way of F**k It.

So just look at your life. Honestly look at what you spend your time doing in the light of whether it is selfish or selfless – or maybe you use other words for now to take away the accustomed meanings of those words: are your actions motivated by self-orientated aims, or with the aim of helping others?

You probably work in order to earn money for yourself (and to give yourself a sense of value, and sometimes to enjoy yourself); you probably spend much of your free time in the pursuit of pleasure for yourself; you go on holiday to satisfy yourself, and so on. Yes, and fair enough too. That's how most of us live.

If you have a family around you and you want to argue that you're not doing things for yourself but for your family, then I'll ask you: why did you start a family in the first place? Wasn't it for yourself? Don't you gain pleasure being with your family? If so, then you're also doing this for yourself.

As normal, 'good' human beings, we are perpetually acting out of self-interest. We're essentially selfish beings. And yet, even as I write that word, there's a charge to it – an implicit:

> *Oh dear, we're not, are we? Well, I'm not, because I always stop for those people on the street who want to sign me up to a life-long direct debit for just what I can afford, which they suggest should be something around £5 a month, which of course doesn't sound much but it all adds up, you know, especially over a lifetime; and it's very difficult for me, you know, to set up a direct debit because my bank prefers me to use the forms they provide, the ones you pick up in the local branch, so, you know, once I just tried to give some real money to the charity, I said: 'Look, I can't do a direct debit just now, but here's £10,' and they said, 'I'm sorry, miss, but we can't take money, we can only do direct debits,' and I thought,* Great, a charity that can't take my money, what's the world coming to? 'Please, miss, I'm starving to death, could you please spare me a direct debit?' *The world's going mad when you can't give money to someone in need...*

So where does this judgement come from? Probably – as usual – from fear. From the fear that if we don't enshrine the concept of selflessness in the heart of our moral code, then we won't give a toss about anyone else – or, more importantly, that no one will give a toss about us when we need it.

But here's the thing: within the whole concept of self-orientated action, of selfishness, is the capacity to help other people. People give money to charity because they feel good about doing so. People help people less fortunate than themselves because it makes them appreciate how lucky they are in their lives. People put themselves out for other people because it gives them a sense of purpose in their lives.

This doesn't reduce the quality of what 'good' people are doing for other people. It just recognizes something in it that most people don't spot.

And it's an important quality to recognize if you ever need to raise money for charity. People are reluctant to just send money off to a cause that will never affect them or their families, and give no 'return' on their money.

This is why campaigns that allow you to 'sponsor an African child' work so well. You get a photograph of the child that you're helping and they write to thank you. This is perfect: you're genuinely helping someone but you're also getting the natural self-orientated satisfaction from doing so.

But here we are again, back in the world of charity. And that takes up only a tiny proportion of our time and money – for most of us, anyway. Let's go back to the family to examine how selfishness versus selflessness works day to day.

When I look at the time I've spent with my family, the only periods I would tag as 'selfless' are those when I'm doing things that I don't really want to be doing. If I'm looking after the boys when I'm dog-tired and they're in a state that doesn't suit me at that moment, then I could well tag my persistence in the task 'selfless'.

I certainly do not want to call the majority of my time with my family 'selfless'. If I'm working to support my family, I do so because I love it that I'm supporting them. If I'm playing on the beach with my boys, I am doing so for myself as much as them: that's not selfless.

So it appears – just in my own family situation – that anything that smacks remotely of 'selflessness' is only the times when we're having trouble. Everything else – all the happy, abundant, laughter-filled times – is self-motivated, as we're all getting what we want.

To be selfless is to sacrifice something you want in favour of something that someone else wants (or needs).

In business, it was once the vogue to talk about 'win-win' situations. Win-win is just one (desirable) outcome of several possible outcomes in any negotiation between two parties.

Let's say I run a hot-dog stall and you own a football club. Now, selling hot dogs outside the ground is strictly illegal. And the police have asked you, the owner of the football club, to help stamp it out. So we're talking, face-to-hot-dog-smelling-face.

TO BE SELFLESS IS TO SACRIFICE SOMETHING YOU WANT IN FAVOUR OF SOMETHING THAT SOMEONE ELSE WANTS (OR NEEDS).

You tell me your position: you've got to help the police. I tell you my position: this is my living and I sell a lot of hot dogs to fans and they like them. You say you have hot dogs inside the ground. I say people want a hot dog as they're hanging around outside the ground, too, while they're waiting for mates, queuing at the turnstiles. You say that if things carry on as they are, you lose: the police will not get off your back until it's sorted out (i.e. I win, you lose). I say that if you cave in to the police, I lose: I'll go out of business. And the fans lose, because they'll lose something that they want (i.e. I lose, you win, but with the unhappy fans, you lose too, anyway).

So we sit there and think. Look, I say, my hot dogs are good. My stall is clean. I'll get the health and safety to give me a check every week. And maybe you can make me an 'official' hot-dog supplier. Okay, you say, that should satisfy the police, that should satisfy the fans, but what about the hot-dog sales I'm losing in the ground? (That was nearly a win-win, but you want your last ounce.)

Okay, I say, if I go 'official' I'll raise my prices by 5 per cent and I'll give you the extra. Though it will have to be cash, mind. And you can trust me: I sell hot dogs.

Deal, you say.

And we shake. And we've just demonstrated a negotiation to a win-win situation.

In any transaction with the world, it's worth getting to a win-win situation. That's where I am with my family. That's where the charity-giver with the photo of his orphan sitting on his desk is. And it's where you can be in every area of your life.

Why should you sacrifice what you want for what others want or need:

* in your relationship?

* with your family?

* in work?

★ with your friends?

★ with people less fortunate than yourself?

If you want, you can start to invent new terms for it, like 'enlightened self-interest' or 'proper selfishness'.

So it's worth saying F**k It to selflessness. If you start to feel you're sacrificing yourself in favour of someone else, then you have to get honing your negotiation skills.

Selflessness is a lose-win situation. And they never work out. You end up getting pissed off, and that's no good in the end for the person who seemed to be winning. It's much better if you think you're getting something out of this relationship too.

SELFLESSNESS IS A LOSE-WIN SITUATION.

The best thing you can do for other people is to put yourself first. Under pressure from the world to be selfless, say F**k It and be selfish.

In the dance of life, pull down your own oxygen mask first, then take a deep breath and help everyone else. They'll thank you for it, believe me.

Say F**k It to Self-control and Discipline

Okay, today I'm going to write the section on self-control and discipline.

But first I'm going to go for a walk and swim. Then I'll have a fruit breakfast. And I won't eat any bread today. And maybe I'll skip dinner tonight. Yes, I'll fast until tomorrow lunch. That should take a bit of this flab off. I was thinking that if I manage to swim every day until my birthday, maybe 50 lengths every day, I'll begin to look a bit better in, well, in my birthday suit.

Maybe that will become a bit tedious, though, doing the same thing every day. I know: I'll walk for an hour one day, then swim the next. And I'll give myself one day off a week. And I'm really going to try to get up before 7 a.m. every day from now on. And the first thing I'll do when I get up is have a cup of hot water with lemon. That's supposed to cleanse the liver. And maybe if I stick to just one glass of wine a night that'll help cleanse the liver, too.

Shit. Almost forgot. What's this section about? Self-control and discipline? Phew, what do I know about that?

What I know is what you know: that our minds love the idea of self-control and discipline. We love the idea of improving, of bettering ourselves, of getting fitter and thinner, or smarter, or more accomplished.

And we think self-control and discipline are always the way. Well, our minds do, anyway. And the above little monologue is what typically goes on in my head. Even though I should know better by now, this is what my mind still gets up to. It just adores the idea of doing something at a certain time, consistently, every day, until some remarkable change has occurred.

So part of the F**k It here is that this stuff will probably be going on in your head *ad infinitum*. You may be lying in a hospital bed, aged 87, unable to move, surrounded by bags to catch your ones and twos, thinking: *If I could just get up and walk to the canteen once a day, I should be able to kick this thing. I could be in shape by Christmas. And I must stop eating that treacle tart, I must ask for the fruit salad instead. That way, I'll be cleansing my intestines and they'll* *get functioning again. And maybe I should ask Derek to bring in those French tapes — it'd be nice to learn a foreign language.*

Or maybe not. Maybe that's the good thing about age. Maybe we learn then what we should all learn much earlier on: it doesn't matter and it's not worth giving a shit.

SAY F**K IT TO IT, AND LET YOUR MIND GET ON WITH IT.

For now, though, let's assume that your mind is going to be doing this stuff a good amount of the time. So say F**k It to it, and let it get on with it. Think of it like a dog playing with a ball in the corner of your garden — just let it play. If it shits on your begonias, then give it a good telling-off, but otherwise let it play.

With the rest of your mind, have a think about this:

The bummer with self-control and discipline is that it doesn't usually work that well, for most of us, anyway. (If you were in the SAS or marines, I suspect you're very good at it and it's worked very well for you — why don't you skip this section? I'm sorry to have bothered you; please don't take offence, it's for other weaker humans, really. Sorry.)

I don't have to tell you how this works. You'll be familiar enough with the numerous abandoned exercise plans, diets and evening classes.

Some people even make a business out of the fact that using our self-control and discipline doesn't work.

I've always wanted to look at the business plan of a big gym like Fitness First (I'm sad like that). I'd love to know what percentage of the people who join up in January they expect to still be coming to the gym by June. It's just a fantastic business idea. You get everyone to sign up to a monthly deal (and getting them to sign away a direct debit is the best way to do this) at the time when everyone's busy sorting out their plans to improve themselves for the year. And within one month, for 80 per cent of them, life has taken over and you'll hardly see them for the rest of the year.

Just get a few more staff in for January, maybe hire a couple more rowing machines, and you're sorted. And you continue to take the £100 a month from their bank account.

The beauty – the absolute genius – of this business is that the 80 per cent of people don't get to mid-February and think: Fuck me, I do this every year. I start with the best of intentions and within four weeks I never see the place again. I'll just cancel my membership today and never be so stupid as to go back there ever again. If I really feel like exercising I'll go outside and have a walk.

What they all say is this: 'I must get back to the gym next week. I haven't been for a couple of weeks now. I shouldn't let it slip. I can't give in. All I need to do is go three times a week, and stop eating… blah, blah, blah.'

Very few people want to stop their £100 a month, because they don't want to admit they've failed. They don't want to admit they have no self-control or discipline. It's an expensive way to make yourself feel slightly better about not exercising. It's like buying a lie: 'I'm a member of a gym so there must be something going on here.'

I'd prefer to buy a badge for £1.50 that I could wear all the time saying: 'I exercise, you know.' Now that's a cheaper way to buy lies.

I'D PREFER TO BUY A BADGE BEARING THE WORDS 'I EXERCISE, YOU KNOW'.

I'm happy to say that – years ago – I did say F**k It to gyms. The moment is very vivid for me. I was on one of those stepping machines. I'd been going this time for a couple of weeks, so was getting rather good on this machine. I was improving on my previous time on every visit, and I'd soon be climbing up the equivalent of Mount Everest every lunchtime.

Then, suddenly, as if there'd been a power-surge that had shot through the stepping machine and straight into my body, I looked around and saw everything with fresh eyes. It all just looked ridiculous: everyone indoors, pretending to be rowing or running or climbing hills or picking up logs. All watching MTV and trying to blank their minds to the absurd reality of what they were doing.

I pressed STOP.

As the two foot-bars of the stepping machine sank gently to the ground, I picked up my water bottle and walked calmly to the changing rooms. I enjoyed my shower, totally at one with myself in the knowledge that I would never set foot in such an absurd place again.

And I haven't.

This section is not sponsored by Fitness First, by the way. Even though I've used their name, I've not endorsed their cause. But I do admire their business plan.

Any attempt you make to control yourself – to impose discipline on yourself – can create some tension. It creates pressure that you usually can't live up to. And the disappointment you face when you can't live up to your own expectations is even more tedious than the frequency with which you let yourself down.

So just say F**k It to it all. Just do what the hell you want. Try not to set up daily tasks for yourself to get fitter or thinner or smarter (though we all still will, of course). Once you lose the tension of these self-imposed expectations, you'll feel so much freer. And when you feel free, you'll be more tuned in to what your body wants:

★ You'll feel like exercising when you feel energetic.

★ You'll feel like vegging out in front of the TV when you don't.

★ You'll feel like eating healthy food sometimes.

★ You'll feel like eating junk at other times.

★ You'll feel like stopping eating when you're full sometimes.

★ And at other times you'll eat until you feel sick.

This is life. Give in to it.

The remarkable thing is that when you give in to the natural flow of life, you'll most probably exercise more than you were doing when you were a member of a gym. And you'll probably eat healthier food overall than when you were seeing that nutritionist. And you'll probably eat smaller portions overall than when you were on some ridiculous diet.

This is how I live. I'm fitter. I'm the same weight. And I keep throwing myself into things like a child. It works for me.

But I don't want you to follow me. That will do you no good at all.

I want you to follow life.

Say F**k It to Plans and Goals

Plans and goals. A goal is the more anal twin brother of the plan. The plan dreams about what he wants to do; the goal then gets really focused and sets some deadlines for achieving these things. They're a very popular team, and lots of people like them and use their services.

Plans and goals are great

I've always been one for making plans and setting goals for myself. I've always been one for making lists of things I need to do and setting goals for different things in my life.

When you decide you want something, whatever it is, it's good to work out a plan for getting it, and to set up some deadlines for getting it done by. It works well.

The problem for a lot of people is that they don't really know what they want. They have vague desires – to 'do something creative' or 'earn more money' or 'be free' – but they can't really pin down what it is precisely that they want. So they drift from one thing to another, enjoying some moments and hating others, but never really finding fulfilment or success (whatever that means to them).

Not really knowing what you want in life is like going into your local DIY store and standing amid the huge aisles of stuff, not knowing what you came for. You wander around for a bit and then go to the information desk. You stand there until someone finally asks, 'Can I help you, sir?' And you look back at them blankly. 'Errrrmmmm… I was looking for… errrrmmm… I was hoping that… errrmmm… I don't really know what I want, actually… Could you recommend something, please?'

It sounds ridiculous.

But that's exactly how a lot of people live their lives. And what happens in their lives is that the woman behind the information desk doesn't just get onto the store PA system and announce, 'Attention, all staff, we have L. Ooney at information; repeat L. Ooney at information. Can we have assistance, please?' No. She actually looks at them with sympathy and says, 'Well, if I were you, I'd start with some paint and a paintbrush. Give your place a bit of a smartening-up, then maybe you can come back later for a drill and some shelves.'

When you don't really know what you want in life, the world can be very sympathetic and throw suggestions your way. But they often have no relevance to what you really need, because no one even knows what they want (like you).

This is why it's hard to lead a successful life (whatever that means to you) when you don't know what you want. A very vague message is sent out to the world, and you get only vague or inappropriate stuff back.

IT'S HARD TO LEAD A SUCCESSFUL LIFE WHEN YOU DON'T KNOW WHAT YOU WANT.

It's a different story, of course, if you go up to the information desk, get out your list and say: 'Good afternoon, could you please take me to find two-inch medial screws, lateral piping, the drill-generator section, and green envelope paint?' (Guess who doesn't do much DIY? Please bear with me.) Assuming that these things exist in the store, after dealing with L. Ooney just now, the assistant is happy to whisk you off to find everything you need.

And this is how the world works. When you're very focused on what you need, the world tends to help you get it.

Doesn't it say in the Bible, 'Ask and ye shall receive'? So, assuming that 'ye' means 'you' rather than some Scottish dude down the road, you're in for a good time if you start making plans (and goals).

Of course, the Bible also says, 'and the goat shall liveth with the man and the man shall be happy', and who needs goats to be happy nowadays? In this day and age, we can all be happy with our blow-up goats. They're far cleaner and, as long as they don't graze near thorn bushes, you're in for a trouble-free relationship.

So don't take everything the Bible says seriously. And that goes for what I say, too. Pick and choose. That's the way to wisdom.

To lead a successful life, then, it's a good idea to work out what you really want. Then get together some plans. Then set some goals. There are plenty of books on these things. So maybe your first plan could be to buy one of these books. And your first goal could be to buy it by Saturday and read it by the following Saturday.

But first read this next bit.

Plans and goals are rubbish

For exactly the reason that plans and goals are good for your life, they're a bummer, too. When you make a plan and set a goal, your life tends to move towards this point. You become very focused on what you're trying to achieve, and life does too. What happens in this global attempt to reach your goal is that you block out all the other possibilities.

Imagine looking at a photograph on your phone of a crowded Trafalgar Square. It's a sunny day and everyone looks as if they're enjoying themselves. But you instantly start to home in on one detail: you use the magnifying facility to begin to focus on just one person – a man who is looking into one of the fountains. He seems lost and unaware of everything that's going on around him. And you continue to magnify down to his right hand. Where you find a tattoo of a peculiar symbol. You stare at that symbol and wonder what it must mean. You print this magnified picture and stick it on your wall to ponder on.

And this is what we do when we focus on something.

No matter how fascinating the thing we focus on, we necessarily exclude all the rest of the stuff. You didn't pause to look at what other people were doing on that day. You didn't notice the reflection of light on the water of the fountain. You didn't spot the levitating dog show (a world premiere), and you didn't spot your wife in a passionate embrace with your best friend.

Every moment has infinite potential. Every new moment contains for you possibilities that you can't possibly imagine. Every day is a blank page that you could fill with the most beautiful drawings.

The problem with a plan is that you fill up the blank page of a new day with a 'to do' list before you get there.

And if you're not careful, there's no room for anything else.

A plan, especially a very focused one, narrows down the possibilities of the future to just a couple of scenarios: that things either go to plan, or they don't (and you're disappointed). This is, of course, why many of us make plans: we're scared of infinite possibility and prefer to live with what we know and what we feel safe with.

A PLAN NARROWS DOWN THE POSSIBILITIES OF THE FUTURE.

But if you can say F**k It to this fear of possibility and unpredictability, your life can really open up.

The way we live our lives is that we drag into each new moment the shit from the past and our limited expectations of the future. We drag into the present all our fears, our judgements, our hang-ups, our limits (of ourselves and others), and previously made plans.

Without any of these things, the moment is just open and ripe. We are free within a free and abundant world that responds to our freedom with unexpected gifts and blessings.

And yes, of course, this section has just contradicted the previous one. First I'm wanting you to make plans, I'm even encouraging you to buy the book… then I'm telling you to abandon plans for a free life.

Trust me. I'm driving. And I know where we're going. So don't scream when I suggest you should…

…say Fk It and take your hands off the steering wheel.**

It's time for a story.

We are on holiday at Butlins, a holiday camp, in Skegness, on England's east coast. I am four. And I am in heaven. I'm sitting inside a small 1930s-style car on a children's track, ready to go. Now, there are times of my life that I can remember exactly: what I was thinking, what I was feeling. And this is one of them.

So the ride begins and off we go. I am so excited. I am driving a car. Just like my dad drives his car, I'm driving a car. And I'm hanging on to the steering wheel ready to prove my abilities as a driver. I come to the first corner – a sharp right – and I carefully and precisely turn the steering wheel to the right. I come to the next corner – a left this time – so I turn the steering wheel to the left.

I am in bliss, I am driving. And I'm doing a good job by all accounts, given this is my first time out on the road/track.

But then a thought crosses my mind. A small thought at first. But it grows in size as I approach the next corner, another right. And I decide to put my thought to the test. As the moment arrives when I have to proficiently swing the steering wheel to the right, I proficiently swing it to the left. I see the risk of flying through the hedge and into the boating pond, but I take it anyway.

And what happens?

The car drives straight round the right bend, of course.

I am gutted. I am dizzy. And I start turning the steering wheel left and right in frustration. I am on a straight, and the steering wheel is turning freely in my hands with absolutely no effect.

I feel cheated beyond belief. Why don't they trust me? I can't understand it.

This feeling was soon to be repeated with the discovery that Santa Claus didn't exist. Then, soon after, that Jesus Christ was just a man with a beard and sandals from the past invented by men with beards and sandals in the present.

For most of us, we've been in that car for 30 or 40 or 50 or 60 (please insert your age minus four or five) years. We've been driving round and round the track, diligently turning at every corner, thinking we're in control. We haven't yet tried taking our hands off the wheel. And we're now so tired that we're dropping off on the straights and shaking ourselves to wake up for the corners. We keep going because we think we have to keep going to stop the car from crashing.

But now it's time to have a go at taking your hands off the wheel. And you'll soon find, like I did as a child, that the car drives itself. Only for you, given you're so knackered, you won't be disappointed at all, you'll be over the moon.

It's time to take your hands off the wheel of life. And you will indeed discover that it runs along quite happily without you doing a great deal. It's time to rest, to put your feet up and sit back and enjoy the ride for a change.

It is a truly remarkable thing, this. And you'll only really get it when you do it. But the moment you stop trying to control and make things happen, everything just happens quite perfectly without you.

IT'S TIME TO REST, PUT YOUR FEET UP AND ENJOY THE RIDE.

In fact, on the surface, little will change. You'll still go about your daily business. You'll still be making decisions to do things. But you'll have this real sense that things are just happening.

In Taoism this is giving in to the natural flow of the Tao. In Scooby Doo, Shaggy would say, 'Go with the flow, man.'

When we sit back more and let things take their natural course, all the tension of 'I must achieve this and do this with my life' evaporates.

I took my hands off the wheel a while back. And the book that I'd been trying to write for a couple of years… the book that I'd set up plans and goals for… well, it just started to write itself.

I write these words because I can't do anything else. No matter how hard I try, I can't do anything else. In fact, that's just a turn of phrase, because I'm not trying hard to do anything, or anything else. I'm just living. And things are just happening very naturally. Including writing this very book. I'm enjoying writing it (for now at least), and I hope you're enjoying reading it.

Sometimes I make plans and goals, sometimes I don't. Sometimes I fulfil them, sometimes I don't. If I don't, sometimes I get upset. Sometimes I don't. This is the flow of life. And no matter what I do, it'll flow just the same.

So, say F**k It to goals and plans. If you're into them, you'll still have them. If you're not into them, you may start making them. But recognize that things will flow as they flow, no matter what you try to do with them.

So, take your hands off the wheel and see what happens.

Say F**k It to Improving

The biggest 'improvement' any of us could ever make is accepting ourselves more, as we are.

And the general wave of invitations to improve – improve our fitness, our eating, our efficiency, our brains, our performance, our habits, our behaviour, our approach, our cooking skills, our dating skills, our improvement skills – all reminds us of one critical thing: ...that we are not good enough (yet) and need to keep improving.

Which is the opposite of the biggest 'improvement' that any of us could make – which is, again, to accept ourselves more, as we are.

So say F**k It to the idea that you have to improve beyond what you are now, because this is not good enough.

Sure, it doesn't mean that you're likely to stop wanting to learn and develop and refine how you are.

But you might be doing it more from a place of self-acceptance and sufficiency rather than the 'I'm not good enough' place of insufficiency.

Say F**k It to Wanting the World to Be a Better Place

No matter how hard people try, the apparent balance between 'good' and 'evil' – between 'peace' and the opposite, fighting and war – always remains pretty much the same. There have always been 'good' people. And there have always been 'bad' people.

> **NO MATTER HOW HARD PEOPLE TRY, THE APPARENT BALANCE BETWEEN 'GOOD' AND 'EVIL' REMAINS PRETTY MUCH THE SAME.**

The effects of good action in the world have been phenomenal. And so have the effects of bad action. The latter just tends to get more news. In fact, the latter tends to get all the news.

Consequently, we tend to think that the world is generally 'bad' and we've got to make it a better place.

And, just as an aside on this news thing, there's a newspaper that sets out to redress the news imbalance: it only gives you positive news. In fact, it's called *Positive News*. It does what it says on the tin. Have you read it? If you haven't, try to find a copy. It's available in all good vegan newsagents. Read it. And see if you can stay awake. You'll be reaching for your regular doom-filled daily before you can say 'paedophile crack dealer in terrorist plot'.

And I'm not dissing all those who pray for peace, fight evil and try to beat the bad guy. I'm also not dissing all those who pray for destruction, fight good and try to beat the good guy. They will both go at each other, tooth and nail, for as long as there are humans.

Sometimes it'll look like the good guy's winning. Sometimes the bad guy. In the end, it all works out the same: they balance each other out over time.

So here's the thing: let's recognize that good will never win out over bad, or vice versa.

Let's accept things as they are... just exactly as they are right now. Let's say F**k It to the battle. It really doesn't matter. The news is the same every day. Just with different names. It's boring.

So just feel what it's like to give up the battle (whichever side you're on). You're not going to win. You're not going to make a difference. Because the final score is always a draw (which is great if you're into the Pools). Give up your desire for the world to be a better place, and do the Pools instead.

What does it feel like? Yes, again, it feels like you're relaxing. It feels like you're lying back. You lose your tight grip on life. You lose your desire for things to be other than they actually are.

Finally resigning yourself to things as they actually are is a real blast. This is the blast of saying F**k It.

RESIGNING YOURSELF TO THINGS AS THEY ACTUALLY ARE IS A REAL BLAST.

Like everything else that you do, once you start saying F**k It, the effect is peculiar. Once you give up wanting the world to be a better place, you may well start actually doing something that has an apparent effect in the world.

It's a bummer, isn't it? But as you're probably beginning to get, it does seem to be true. If you're not beginning to 'get', just F**k It anyway.

Say F**k It to Being Uptight

Time for another story from when we were still living in Italy (we now live back in the UK).

I've just got back from the local post office (in Urbino, Italy). As I was waiting in line, there were two customers in front of me and two at the desks, and three members of staff behind the desks, two of them dealing with customers, the other doing some paperwork.

And the one doing the paperwork was clearly really miffed with the employee next to her: 'I can't come here in the morning and have to deal with this kind of problem; it's not up to me,' she said to him. The guy was giving as good as he was getting: 'That happens to be your job, so why on Earth can't you just do it?'.

'Well, it was never made clear to me that I would have to deal with this kind of problem...' And so on.

These two were not holding back, despite the fact there were customers present, and another member of staff. They were just bickering, like an old couple. Nothing vicious, just gentle bickering. And it made me feel uncomfortable. I couldn't understand why they didn't just hold it back; save it until later. But there seemed to be no awareness that this wasn't a great thing to be doing: having a public argument, especially in front of customers. I looked around. No one else – customers or staff – seemed be uncomfortable: I don't know whether they'd even noticed what was happening.

And then I remembered something: we're in Italy, and I'm English.

In England, we *do* hold it back. We're polite even when we're seething. We save it until later, and that later often never comes. We keep it in and push it down. Not so here in Italy. I've lived here for years now but it clearly hasn't sunk in at a deeper level that this is what people do.

Years ago, I'd constantly implore Gaia and her mum to stop arguing. They'd pause, look at me in surprise, and say: 'We're not arguing, we're just talking'. Well, it bloody well looked like arguing to me: raised voices, overt gesticulations.

But then I saw that people here do indeed raise their voices and gesticulate dramatically, even when they're just talking about the weather (which they do, it's not just us Brits. Although they talk more about food. Brits talk incessantly about the weather, while Italians talk incessantly about food, usually whenever they're eating food).

So, those two post office employees were having a barney, and they weren't bothered about who heard it. And the people who heard it weren't bothered about hearing it. It didn't feel great to me, but maybe it was: she was telling him that she wasn't happy, he was listening, and then saying his piece too.

Clear, honest communication. Nothing held back. They didn't come to blows. They'll probably work it out.

I'm getting used to this kind of communication (though clearly not completely, or this morning's episode wouldn't have made me feel uncomfortable). And when I go back to the UK, which I do fairly regularly, I'm struck by how much people hold back when they're talking. We communicate, generally, in a polite way, even when we're trying to express something difficult.

We'd never say something difficult *outright*, so we try to make it clear without actually *saying* it. Yes, I know, madness. Therefore, we've become adept at reading between the lines of any conversation. Here's an example:

You get on well with the couple next door and their children, but the son plays loud music late into the evening and it disturbs you. If you're British, though, the next time you're invited over to their house for a glass of wine, you don't just come out with it: 'Your son's music is a little too loud for us in the evening... it's fine during the day, but it's too much in the evening. Could you ask him to keep it down, please?'

No, first you spend a long time deliberating over how to broach the subject. Then you work out ways to drop hints into the conversation. You might, for example, start talking about some other family and refer to their son as a tearaway who's up all night taking drugs and terrorizing the neighbourhood with his loud music. By exaggerating the story, you make it clear that you're not talking about *them*, but it'll certainly make them wonder whether their son's music is a problem for you.

Or you invent something. Maybe you say that you've been suffering from headaches recently, and that you've become very sensitive to noise – so much so that you can't bear your daughter doing her piano practice. When the neighbours say, as they probably will, 'Oh, I hope our son's music is not disturbing you,' you'll even exclaim, 'Oh no, I wasn't saying *that* (even though you were), I'm just finding any loud noises difficult.' Your neighbours then get the point and talk to their son.

It is madness, but it's how it's done.

It means, though, that you're always wondering what people are actually trying to say. You never know whether something is genuine or just some padding to something that's more difficult to express.

In business, there's even a dreadful expression for this: the 'shit sandwich'. If you have something difficult to say to someone – such as, 'You're not doing well enough' – you start off by saying some nice stuff about them: 'We're all very happy with how you're getting on.' That's the first slice of bread. Then you hit them with the shit: 'That said, we think you could do better in this area.' Then you complete this charming sandwich with another slice of soft bread: 'But, overall, we're all very happy with you.'

Bullshit.

What this means is that no one trusts what anyone says any more. When someone pays you a compliment, you're always waiting for the 'but, that said' that comes afterwards.

This means that the UK is, generally, more uptight than somewhere like Italy. Because it's hard to say stuff openly, we either don't say it (suppress it), or we struggle to find a way to say it. And on the receiving end, we struggle to work out what the hell everyone's trying to say to us.

For example, you pop into the baker's one morning and are greeted by Sarah Wiggins. 'My, you're looking very well,' she says, 'really got some colour in your cheeks.' And you're left wondering what it is that she's *really* saying. Is she saying that you usually look ill and pale? Is she implying, somehow, that you're melancholic? Does she suspect you're depressed? Christ.

Last night, I was talking to someone who said that they have trouble even *going* into uptight places, which in their case is London. They said that they can't help but take on all that uptightness and tension themselves, and so they prefer just to stay away.

So how can *you* remain free in Uptight Town?

Well, I think it can actually be a rather pleasant experience. It serves to remind you how free, relaxed and clear you are when you're suddenly surrounded by people who are uptight, tense and suppressed. If you do feel the uptightness pushing in on you, then simply use it as training. Ask yourself: 'How can I remain conscious and relaxed in this uptight atmosphere?'

I actually *like* being around very uptight people sometimes, because it reminds me how well I'm doing. Occasionally I have uptight people bussed into my home – where they storm around being stressed – because it relaxes me so much. They should do that as a service, shouldn't they? (And of course, I have no idea who I mean by 'they'… you know, 'they'; 'thems who sorts things'). They should offer to ship in people who are worse off than you in any difficult situation.

ASK YOURSELF: 'HOW CAN I REMAIN CONSCIOUS AND RELAXED IN THIS UPTIGHT ATMOSPHERE?'

Feeling sick? We'll send in half a dozen people who are more sick, much more sick, than you are. You'll feel better instantly.

Feeling anxious? We'll send you a couple of people who are so anxious that we had to drag them out of their homes in handcuffs to get them here. You'll feel as peaceful as the Dalai Lama when you see these two, believe us.

Feeling uptight and suppressed? We'll send you to England for a long weekend. My, will you feel liberated, relaxed and clear over there in comparison to that lot.

It is possible to be free and relaxed and clear in Uptight Town: you say F**k It and embrace it, and you'll most likely feel better yourself when you realize how much more relaxed and clear you are than everyone around you.

Say F**k It to Searching

We're all searchers. We're always looking for more meaning. The search is relatively unconscious for much of our life. We search for meaning in relationships, in friendships, in jobs, in money, in hobbies, in 'missions' to help other people.

We're very lucky in Western society, because many people have unparalleled opportunities to get what they want. There's more freedom and fluidity of work, of movement, of belief, of sexuality, of gender than there has ever been.

WE'RE ALL SEARCHERS. WE'RE ALWAYS LOOKING FOR MORE MEANING.

So, in your search for meaning and satisfaction, you can get to the place you're after relatively quickly. For those who think that true meaning and satisfaction lie in getting their dream job, or finding their dream lover, or owning a BMW, if they really put their mind to it, they can actually achieve it.

What tends to happen, though, is once the object is achieved or owned, we then move on to the next thing. And the next, and the next.

If this happens often enough, people get to the point where they think to themselves, *There must be more to life than this.* And they tend to get spiritual. This is great. This is why it's a blessing to be rich and successful – it means you get to the point of realizing riches and success don't mean a lot more quickly than those that don't have them.

This, of course, doesn't mean that only rich and successful people have the wisdom to get spiritual. It's just one example of an area of search. If you think that meaning and satisfaction reside in your sexual conquests, then it's a blessing if you get to shag enough people to realize that 'there must be more to life than this'.

If you think that meaning and satisfaction reside in your spotting every train in the UK, one by one (i.e. trainspotting), then it's a blessing if you get to spot them all as quickly as possible so you too can get to realize that 'there must be more to life than this'.

For whatever reason, people get spiritual apparently towards the end of their pursuit of meaning.

And nowadays, 'spiritual' means a whole supermarket of possibilities. Previously in the UK, there was just a corner shop at the end of your street that sold the same thing to everyone: Spam. And Christianity was the Spam of the past. Sure, you could add Spam to other things to get a slightly different twist: Spam with chips, Spam with eggs, Spam in mashed potato, even Spam with Spam. Just as there are Protestants and Catholics and Jehovah's Witnesses. But they're all still Spam with a twist.

Nowadays shopping is a huge out-of-town affair with every possible food catering for all possible tastes – ethnic, ready-meal, frozen, etc. And similarly, we can choose from all the different organized religions – Christianity, Judaism, Islam, Hinduism – or the ones that look like religions – Buddhism – or the ones that are structured, but nothing like religions: yoga, shamanism, Taoism.

What many people tend to do, of course, is go to the pick'n'mix counter. They take a scoopful of yoga, add a bit of Buddhism, have a little taste of Taoism, a sprinkle of the latest wisdom vogue, maybe mindfulness, a bit of *The Power of Now*, some New-Age philosophies about abundance and karma, and so on.

Of course, they don't buy any meat, and sometimes no dairy produce, and often bypass the bread, too (there I go a-mixing the metaphors again), but off they go to the checkout with a whole basket-full of stuff.

And now supermarkets sell things they never used to: clothes, books, toys. And this is the world of alternative therapy. From a regular massage to Chinese medicine and Reiki and homoeopathy – these extras all have a spiritual edge that becomes part of your new belief system, even if it's as basic as, 'I believe massage helps to calm me down.'

In the olden days, if you went to the corner shop and bought a tin of Spam and some potatoes, there was a good chance the next person would buy the same thing. That's how belief and religion were, too: we were all doing practically the same thing.

Today, if you look at the baskets and trolleys going through the checkouts, you'll see that no two are the same. They're packed full of a huge variety of goods. And for most of us, that's how it is with our belief systems, too: they're different from each other, and relatively complicated.

But at one very basic level, nothing has changed: belief and spirituality are very meaningful. And, to many people, they're everything.

And as we already know, meaning creates tension and pain when it comes into conflict with what life is. So the more meaningful your belief/spirituality/religion is, the more potential for tension and pain:

★ If you believe it's wrong to have sex before marriage, then every moment of lust and desire will drive you mad.

★ If you believe it's wrong to be gay, then gay people will make you tense and judgemental.

★ If you believe in abundance, then giving away your money and not getting 10 times in return will piss you off.

★ If you believe in the power of peace over all, then wars will upset you.

★ If you believe that the meek shall inherit the Earth, then it makes you angry to see the powerful and rich having a good time in the meantime.

★ If you believe a woman should cover herself up from head to toe, then any revealed female flesh will make you angry.

★ If you believe that God will have His day, then you don't appreciate this day as much.

★ If you believe the powers of evil should be crushed, you might commit acts of 'evil' to achieve this.

★ If you believe the answer lies in the afterlife, you miss the answers in this life.

★ If you believe in past lives, you can give up responsibility for your present one.

★ If you believe that Jesus will return to save you, you forget that there's nothing to save you from.

★ If you believe that non-judgement is the way to peace, your own judgement causes you pain and guilt.

So here's another cosmic joke: the search in our lives leads us to try to find meaning beyond what 'is' in our lives. Our loves, our money, our achievements are not quite enough, so we look for more. And we ultimately look for it in 'spirituality', which usually involves the 'unseen' (which you could say is what 'isn't').

The question for the seeker is thus this: what if this were it? What if the answer is here, now, under my nose: that I don't need to go anywhere or do anything, or learn anything new, or become anyone else, or improve, or purify?

When we say F**k It to the search, we also say: F**k It, This Is It.

Say F**k It and Give Stuff Away

Yesterday we were in our favourite bakery/deli in Hove, Brod+Wolf, choosing some loaves (but not fishes), and Jess, who was serving us, said, 'I don't know how you say it – "*meel foglier*", I think – but would you like a free pastry? You'll find it in the fridge.'

And I went to the fridge and there was the most delicious-looking, delicate *mille foglie* pastry – which is lots of layers (though not a thousand, as the name suggests) of pastry, cream, fruit and other things that taste sweet and amazing (and that I later found out was made by their chef Rosie) – with a sign in front of it bearing a heart symbol and the word 'free'.

And I cradled this delicate creation and took it to the promenade and sat on a bench and ate it while looking out to sea, the saltiness of the air mixing beautifully with the gentle sweetness of the pastry and the gesture.

Now, a *mille foglie* pastry is best eaten on the day it's made. That's one reason they were giving it away. But they were still *giving* it away: they weren't reducing the price, or throwing it away or feeding the birds.

And you don't see that very often. With businesses in particular. They only usually give you something if they figure it will mean you'll buy something expensive as your next purchase (like insurance).

Generosity amongst friends and family is somewhat different.

We're lucky enough to know some really generous people.

Just about whenever we meet our friend Mark, he has a bag with something in it for us, a cake he's made

THEY WERE GIVING IT AWAY AND YOU DON'T SEE THAT VERY OFTEN.

(he knows we have a thing for cake), or a box of pencils (he knows I have a thing for pencils), or some tins of craft beer (he knows… oh, you get the picture of me and my things).

And there's not a day goes by without us muttering some words of gratitude to our friend Mandy. The quick backstory is that we moved from Italy back to the UK in 2019 and we knew we wouldn't be able to bring all our stuff straight away. We had just a car-full of stuff – clothes and essentials – but the rest went into storage.

So we needed a whole range of stuff to help us live a comfortable life.

Gaia had this idea: why don't we ask Mandy if she could help fill our house, if she'd be happy asking around to see whether people had things they didn't need that could help us out. But the thought embarrassed me. It would put Mandy out. People might give things that they actually needed, but felt obliged to help… and so on.

I felt uncomfortable just thinking about it. The kind of uncomfortable you'd feel if you had a large empty lounge with nothing to sit on, which was actually the situation we were in. Funny that.

So Gaia asked Mandy, and they chatted a lot about what we'd need.

And a month later, we hired a van with two guys who moved all the stuff that had been donated and accumulated from Mandy's garage into our house. And it didn't take long for me to realize that we'd have been up the creek without a paddle (or a comfy armchair for that matter) without Mandy's help.

Mandy is naturally a generous person. Incredibly generous. So much so that we all have to watch that we don't take too much of her generosity of time, spirit and, in this case, 'things'.

And what 'things' arrived in that van.

Mandy had thought of everything.

And her army of family and friends had heeded the call.

So I am currently sitting at a table that was once sat around by Mandy and her beautiful family.

I'm looking over at a cool sofa that used to be in her son Steven's cool hair salon, Gilded Pleasure, in Arundel.

I will later be binge-watching some Scandinavian *noir* on the huge flatscreen smart TV that her daughter Abbi donated. There's a set of drawers from her son Stuart, a bed from her mum, a set of chairs from one of her friends.

Mandy filled our empty kitchen with pots and pans, knives and forks, plates and cups, tea towels, oven gloves and whatever else goes in a kitchen – all from her own kitchen.

We light the house with numerous gorgeous lamps from Mandy's.

I have a Buddha on my desk here: Mandy's.

Yup, wherever I look, wherever I sit, when I lie to sleep, or sup a drink or eat at a table from a plate with a fork, I'm reminded of Mandy's (and her family and friends') deep generosity.

And I have to say, despite my initial discomfort, receiving such (almost) overwhelming generosity has been good for me.

It's been good to receive.

But my, look how good it is to give.

Please do give when you can. If you're not quite sure, if you're wondering about whether you should hold onto something, whether you might need that one day (though certainly not today), say F**k It and give.

Say F**k It to More

It all started 300 years ago not far from where I was born (in the Midlands of England).

People came in from the fields and started making stuff that they and their community needed, from their cottages.

Later, they went off to factories in which the stuff that people around the world needed would be made in a fraction of the time and cost (aka the 'Industrial Revolution').

And because of this, more people could afford more stuff, so more factories opened and even more stuff was made.

There were a couple of pauses in this development, when the factories switched from making more stuff that people didn't really need to making stuff that would kill people who had decided they wanted more land and more power and not just more stuff.

But soon they were back to making the stuff that people didn't really need.

And they found ever ingenious ways to persuade people that they needed things that they didn't, even if they could hardly afford what they didn't need.

They were able then to borrow more money to buy more things that they didn't really need, but to afford all this stuff and the repayments on the loans to buy all this stuff, they had to travel more to find more work, and work more hours.

SOON THEY WERE BACK TO MAKING THE STUFF THAT PEOPLE DIDNT REALLY NEED.

And the more they worked and the more they travelled and the more they consumed, the more they polluted the planet, until more strange weather events started happening, and the more particles of chemicals and plastic got into people's bodies, the more sick they became, until they couldn't really work any more.

Enough.

Start today.

Say F**k It to More.

And embrace enough.

It's one obvious way to break the cycle of more.

Say F**k It to Emojis

Talking of saying F**k It to more, emojis are a daily example to me of 'just because you can, it doesn't mean you should'.

I've been using two or three 'emojis' for many years. Including the long-gone time when you could type in colon-dash-close-brackets and what would appear is something that looked like a smiling face on its side. I literally can't do that here now, because when I try:

It turns it into a smiley face, right way up – no nose, but clearly still very happy.

Editor, can you find a way to put an original smiley in here please?

:-)

Ahhh, how cool is that? Such a pity we can't use emojis like that any more...

Sad face here please:

:-(

Actually reader, I just figured out how to do that on my own. You just keep trying and it eventually leaves the original characters:

;-)

Now, I can argue – and I will – that those three keyboard-character-created emojis and their omnipresent enforced-on-us yellow-faced descendants can aid communication.

It is easy to be ambiguous in an email. It's often hard to convey tone and nuance, so a little emoji can help.

> I could punch you in the face for suggesting that ☺

…then tends to be interpreted as an assumption that you're kidding (though maybe a little offended) rather than a genuine threat.

> I'm sorry I can't be with you on your birthday ☹

…does add some emotion (probably genuine) to what could otherwise be a rather formal and emotionless statement.

Of course you can hide behind emojis too:

> You're not answering my calls. If you're still in bed, it's probably time you got up you lazy good-for-nothing piece of poo ☺

But, overall, I appreciate the clarity emojis bring and the emotion they can convey.

But the rest of them… ☹

What market imperative has driven the multiplication of these little symbols?

On the rare occasions that I've tried to find an appropriate emoji for something (e.g. on a birthday, and I'm trying to find a cake or balloons or poppers or anything, because I couldn't be bothered to buy the actual things in real life), I've had to scroll through reams of useless stuff, like modes of transport, or types of drink, or whatever.

I usually give up and just type – or 'swipe', as I'm most likely to do on my phone – 'Hope you have a great birthday'.

The thing is, since I thought about writing a chapter called 'Say F**k It to Emojis', which is generally 'just don't use emojis because they're a waste of time and who cares for a little symbol of a unicorn anyway?', my phone now *suggests* emojis for lots of common words.

If I were now to write 'birthday' on my phone, a little birthday cake would pop up as a suggestion alongside other similar words.

And it's so easy to tap that birthday cake.

And look how pretty my previously letter-heavy text now looks.

And oh how funny and delightful my reader will find my text.

And maybe they'll even think I'm smart and attentive for finding such appropriate emojis.

And before long I've fallen into the hole (hole emoji here please, editor), got caught in the trap (animal-cage-like trap here please, editor), been drawn to the rocky shore by the sirens of the emojis (editor, do you reckon they'll have an emoji for the sweet-singing-half-bird-half-human sirens of *The Odyssey*, and if they do, do you think people will get it, or just think I'm up my own bottom – oof, please don't try to find an emoji for that, lol ☺ lol).

Okay, I have on this journey of argument (Odyssey if you will) returned, Homer-like, to home: please say F**k It to emojis, except the ones you can create using your own keyboard.

;-)

Don't Say F**k It to Cheat the Gods

I've shared with you about my healing story: it was the giving up of my huge desire to get well that finally allowed the healing journey to happen.

I've suggested many times in these pages that it's the easing off, and the caring less, the taking of the hands off the wheel, that allows things to start flowing and working more.

With health, for example, when you care less – or maybe not at all – it doesn't mean you necessarily stop eating well or exercising or meditating, or even having acupuncture; but the desperation and investment in doing these things disappears.

I now eat well because I really like the taste of fresh vegetables and fruit. I also like the taste of ice cream, though, so I eat that too.

I now exercise because I really love the feeling of screaming down a hill on a mountain bike, and the sense of physical tiredness in my body… not because it will (one day) contribute to my reaching full, whole health.

I now meditate for the energy that spreads through my body when I do so, but to me, it feels no different from the energy that spreads through my body when I get angry.

What happens, then? As usual, it's all down to relaxation. I – like many people – recognized the power of relaxation to cure illness a long time ago. I trained in Tai Chi and Chi Kung to use movement, breathing and *chi* to totally relax my body. I trained in hypnotherapy to use the mind to totally relax myself. I've tried just about every method of relaxation that's available. Because I knew a long time ago something that a lot of people don't realize: problems have trouble existing in the face of total relaxation.

Physical, mental, emotional, and spiritual problems have little to stick to in the face of total relaxation.

I knew this. I practised the methods to a high level. And yet little changed. Why? Because I still had aims, attachments and myriad meanings. And these are all basically tension. The bummer is this: if you want health and you use even the best relaxation method to try to get it, your very wanting of that health is a tension that the method is unlikely to be able to break down.

So the most advanced relaxation method you'll ever find is not caring and not wanting… saying F**k It.

Give up wanting anything, and everything will come. The thing is, you can't cheat the gods: you can't employ this 'not wanting' thing in order to get what you actually want. The gods (and life) are smarter than that.

GIVE UP WANTING ANYTHING, AND EVERYTHING WILL COME.

Say F**k It and Live Like a LEGEND

I like to mix it up. F**k It, who says we need to be consistent?

I've written about being 'ordinary' and enjoying it.

Well, I also like to live like a legend too.

I like framing peculiar things from my life as if they're valuable memorabilia from a legendary life.

I'm in the process of framing a page from the back of a Sunday magazine. I'll tell you why. For the whole of my life, the backs of Sunday magazines have contained ridiculous adverts for old people. They'd have adverts for peculiar gardening implements, stair lifts, expensive cruises, mobility scooters and so on.

Then last week, I was flicking through a Sunday magazine and found myself avidly reading a full-page advert for a food-delivery service that featured EXACTLY the types of food I like. It's almost as if they were reading my mind (or belly). What's more, there was 30 per cent off my first order AND a free bottle of Italian wine. Were these people CRAZY? Surely they couldn't be making money on that deal!

Then my eyes momentarily darted from the picture of the steak pie to the facing page, where there was an image of an elegant desk-top light, designed for reading. And haven't I been saying recently that I'm struggling to read in low light at my desk? I have to point five lights at anything in order to see it. This lamp had been designed by a team of scientists, engineers and optometrists particularly and specifically to help with reading. And it was only £99, payable in three instalments. And at that very minute I'd have been happy to pay so much more, in one instalment, to solve my low-light reading issue. Surely they couldn't be making money on that offer!

And at that moment I realized something with a jump. The adverts at the back of the Sunday magazines are now aimed at me – targeted so carefully at me that it felt uncanny and the purchases were practically irresistible.

I'd somehow passed from being someone who laughed at the advertisers confined to the back of these magazines for their out-of-touch, crappy, old-fogey products… to being someone who was probably being laughed at by these advertisers as I bit on their bait-covered hooks.

But I regained my power and self-esteem when I decided to memorialize this moment forever by framing the very advert that denoted this precise moment in my life – the moment when I, John C. Parkin, was caught by the Sunday magazine adverts, but was then able to laugh at myself for it.

My, what a LEGEND I am.

And you, my friend, are a legend too.

Just let the scales of mediocrity drop from your eyes and recognize the absolute legendariness of your life. Then go online and buy some picture frames, and off you go.

What legend will you start to celebrate?

> **MY, WHAT A LEGEND I AM. AND YOU, MY FRIEND, ARE A LEGEND TOO.**

Is it the inspiration you felt in the corner shop, when you felt Lady Luck looking down on you, and you bought a scratchcard, only to find you'd won nothing? Frame the card.

Is it the ready-made lasagne for two that you heated up, had for dinner, left a bit, and then finished for breakfast the following morning? LEGEND. Frame the label.

Is it the best man's speech that got you into big trouble with your mate's parents at his wedding? Total legend. Frame it.

Is it the sniffy rejection letter you got for that job you didn't really want? Burn the corner of it, then frame it, you legend.

F**k It, I'm a fucking legend. You're a fucking legend. We got here, we're amazing, we're fucked-up, messy, totally unique human beings. WE ARE LEGENDS.

PART 4

SAYING F**K IT WHEN YOU CAN'T SAY F**K IT

Over the years since the first version of this book hit the bookshelves, I've been asked many times, by journalists and by readers and by people attending our retreats and workshops:

'But aren't there things you can't say F**k It to?'

This question will arise after that person has done a mental checklist of all the things in their life that they'd like to say F**k It to. They happily go ticking down the list: 'Sure, I can say F**k It to my current really strict diet, yup to saying F**k It to going to my parents for Christmas, F**k It to not speaking up in meetings, yes, I can say F**k It and tell my friend how much she hurt me…' and so on.

But then they start to slow down as it gets more tricky.

And they might well start to get frustrated too. Even angry: 'Of course I can't say F**k It to my job, I've got three kids to support, what a ridiculous thing to suggest.' Or critical: 'Suggesting that we can say F**k It to the current humanitarian crisis in _____ is highly irresponsible.' Or self-critical: 'This is agony; I just can't say F**k It to this, so here I am failing again.'

So, saying F**k It, as you most likely understand it (which is usually to care *less* about something), is akin to having the ability to relax: it works a treat in the majority of situations. There aren't many areas of your life that wouldn't benefit from you saying F**k It to them, just as there aren't many areas of your life that wouldn't benefit from you applying some serious relaxation skills.

But there are times, and situations, when – no matter how good you are at relaxation – it doesn't touch it. It's likely that our nervous system is so activated that the relaxation can't get through. And, in some situations, that's a good thing. It's good that we're activated, in fight-or-flight mode for example, when there's a threat. And to relax out of that would not be a good idea. It's difficult, though, when the threat, or the perception of a threat, persists for a sustained period of time.

And there are times, and situations, when, no matter how good you are at saying F**k It, it doesn't touch it, or it's not even appropriate in the first place. Not in the way you probably understand it (which, as I've said, is usually to care less about something). Of course you can't say F**k It if someone you love dearly is dying. Of course you can't say F**k It if you're in physical agony.

Now, I know, it's difficult to contemplate these really difficult things. Most of us want to put our hands over our ears and say, 'Don't talk about that, don't talk about that'. But there will be those of you who are desperate to read this section because, well, about one thing or another you're desperate, and in pain (emotional or physical), and the last thing you can do is say F**k It.

THE LAST THING YOU CAN DO IS SAY FK IT.**

Saying F**k It When You Can't Say F**k It to 'First World Problems'

Ooohh, don't get me started on this one. And I write that imagining Sean Lock saying it (he's the British comedian who died in the summer of 2021). You don't know him? Look him up and laugh the rest of the day away. And then feel sad because he's not here any more. And we'll discuss death and dying soon.

I grew up, often in physical pain or discomfort, often in emotional pain or discomfort, being told that there are so many people in the world much worse off than me. I was told to laugh and the world laughs with you, cry and you cry alone. Ouch.

After a rather happy time at university, I returned home (for a few months, it turned out). I became ill, and wasn't happy. I didn't know what I was going to do with my life. I couldn't see a way through or out. I thought I'd be ill forever.

I sat at the kitchen table one morning with my mum. And I shared how I was feeling. I said I felt terrible and I started crying. And she couldn't take it. She encouraged me to cheer up, telling me that it wasn't so bad. And I swore: 'for f**k's sake'. And she was furious that I'd sworn at her. She was upset not that I was upset, or that she'd offered up such an inadequate and unsympathetic response to my upset, but that I'd sworn in her presence.

I share this because, in the following years, as much as I was able to feel my difficult feelings, and open up to others about my pain, there was always a part of me that was thinking that I was spoiled, that there were so many people in worse situations than me, and that I should just pull myself together.

And it's with huge relief that I'm writing now, when it's so much easier for us all to talk about mental health issues. When celebrities are fine to talk about their mental health challenges. When athletes at the Olympics are openly talking about their fears and struggles. When even members of the royal family are talking about their own struggles with mental health.

And maybe the emergence of a more open debate about mental health issues came at just the right time: just before we humans became more aware of the climate emergency, and its existential threat and the accompanying anxiety that that awareness brought; and just before we humans faced the other existential threat of the global pandemic (starting early 2020), when the effect on people's mental health was part of the debate from the beginning.

Against this backdrop, of increasing openness about mental health issues, and the suggestion that 'it's okay not to be okay', we have the phrase – gggrrrrrrr – 'first world problems'. Which, I have to admit, packs a lot into three words. So I applaud its concision. The copywriter (of short, pithy but evocative lines) in me takes his hat off to that one. Because in just three words you get to say, 'What are you lot complaining about, you snowflakes (another evocative and bile-full term)? There are people out there who are *really* suffering, and you're upset about that? It makes me sick.'

And what you're meant to feel is, 'Oh goodness, you're right, I should just be grateful for what I have, and stop complaining. How silly of me, sorry. Yes, it was very self-indulgent and rather spoilt, and I'll try to put a brave face on it all, and pull myself together, sorry.'

So, first off, let's adjust our profanity. If someone ever says 'first world problems' to anything you say, just reply calmly 'F**k off'. If you need to elaborate, switch up to 'F**k right off'.

If they've even got a 'first world problems' look on their face, take a picture of them, then send them that photo with the accompanying caption: F**k right off.

Here's the thing: there's no international sliding scale of suffering that dictates how we should feel based on what challenges we've faced.

We have the absolute right to feel how we feel. And when those feelings are of pain, we shouldn't have to load shame and guilt on top of those feelings, just for feeling those feelings.

WE HAVE THE ABSOLUTE RIGHT TO FEEL HOW WE FEEL.

Suffering is not a competition. But it seems like the most competitive elements of our 'first world society' have, ironically, recruited the concept that it is, in order to denigrate their 'first world colleagues' who are suffering and being open about it.

I'm sharing things in this book that, most people would agree, even the 'first world problems' arseholes would find pretty challenging. Sure, not starvation. Or torture. But challenging nonetheless.

But, at some level, I'd prefer to share more mundane things in my life that have caused me distress and anxiety, rather than some of the more 'headline' struggles. Growing up, I was more affected and traumatized by something a school-friend said to me than by something that happened to me that would nowadays involve the police (and, yes, would make headlines).

Just over these last couple of weeks, I've been in pain over the shocking daily news from Afghanistan (following the withdrawal of the troops that have been there for 20 years, the Taliban have taken over and there's been a race to evacuate people from the country through Kabul airport, with desperate and heartbreaking scenes, including a bomb attack, around that airport). But I've also been in mundane pain over how to write this section of the book. I know it matters so much. I really want to help those of you who are struggling and in pain, facing things that 'you can't say F**k It to'.

I really want to convey this point – that you have the right to feel what you feel – in a powerful way that gets past all the 'first world problems' bullshit.

I've been waking up in the middle of the night and scribbling notes about it. I've then been struggling to get down to the task of writing it all down (like this, yes, here I am, finally). I've been dreaming about what to write. I've become so worried – that I'm not up to it, that I can't get across what I'm feeling inside, that I'll be criticized for this or that, that it won't be clear enough, or resonant enough, or will contain references that you won't get, or I won't make it by the (extended) deadline, or a hundred things – that I wake up feeling worried and shaky.

And even now, in my head, there's: 'Ooohhh, the writer's there in his comfortable chair at his comfortable desk, worried and shaky about missing his deadline and not 'conveying' his thoughts and feelings adequately, oh poor little snowflake. That's first world problems for you.'

But I have the right to feel how I feel, without judgement, or self-judgement.

And having the right to feel how we feel, without judgement, or self-judgement, is at the core of how to 'say F**k It when we can't say F**k It'.

Saying F**k It When You Can't Say F**k It to Feeling Down

I had lots of alternatives to 'feeling down' for the title of this chapter: 'when you're feeling terrible', 'when you're struggling', 'feeling flat', to list just a few.

We're not, for now, going to look at the likely cause of this feeling, and sometimes there is no likely cause, or there's just a build-up of stuff that's been eating away at you. But the feeling is there. You're down, flat, worried, anxious, struggling, overwhelmed. And there's no saying F**k It to it. You can't say, 'Oh, F**k It to this, I'll just feel another way.'

That's as useless a suggestion as 'just pull yourself together' or 'just snap out of it', which I heard a lot when I was growing up. Generations of people trying (and failing) to pull themselves together. Great.

So here's the F**k It when you can't say F**k It. This is F**k It Advanced if you like. It's: 'F**k It, this is how I'm feeling now.'

Sounds simple, eh? Well, just try it next time you're feeling flat, or you're struggling.

It's more difficult than it sounds, because everything in us is trying *not* to feel those feelings. Which is natural of course; these are painful feelings.

But try to say F**k It to all the sirens of distraction. It's usually easier to get distracted by our phones, or watch the TV, or have a drink, or eat too much, or throw ourselves into work, or get pulled into some drama in our relationships.

It's easier, too, to blame others for how we're feeling. We might not do it consciously, but we walk out of the front door and start complaining about the world, and judging and criticizing people, and tutting and moaning about how things are. When all we're doing is avoiding looking at how things really are inside us.

It's easier, too, to have an action plan for pulling ourselves together: to go out for walks, eat better, get enough sleep, talk to friends, and so on. And such things do usually help.

But don't let anything distract from saying: 'F**k It, this is how I'm feeling now'; 'F**k It to everything that's pulling me away from these difficult feelings'; and 'this is how I'm feeling' to whatever I'm feeling.

By saying this, we sit with the difficulty and the struggle.

By saying this, we look the pain straight in the eyes.

It's not easy, we have to keep breathing. But with practice it becomes easier.

'F**k It, this is how I'm feeling now.'

Use it as a mantra. It is your route into more acceptance of what is, not how you'd like things to be, but what is – at the most essential level – how you're feeling, now.

So, what happens then?

Well, that part of you then feels heard. And allowed. That in itself helps.

Imagine a child who is scared and upset. The loving parent will hold them and listen to them, not dismiss their feelings. The loving parent will say they understand and reassure the child. The child then learns to feel safer having such feelings and expressing such feelings.

When we say 'F**k It, this is how I'm feeling now,' we're saying to ourselves that it's safe to feel like this, and sit in this, no matter how difficult it is.

And if you still find yourself being pulled away from, and resisting, difficult feelings, I'll remind you of this: we all feel fragile at times, we all struggle at times, we all feel down, overwhelmed, worried, anxious at times. You are not alone.

One of the most healing aspects of the retreats we do is hearing other people sharing their own struggles and realizing, 'Ahh, I'm not alone; they're feeling what I'm feeling.'

So, we are not alone, in that many others are feeling just as we are.

SO, WE ARE NOT ALONE, IN THAT MANY OTHERS ARE FEELING JUST AS WE ARE.

And we are not alone in that there's plenty of help out there when we really need it.

Because part of the process of saying 'F**k It, this is how I'm feeling now', is to recognize when we need to speak to others, or ask others, including professionals, for help.

If you do recognize that, and there's a voice in your head resisting it, it's time to say another 'F**k It' and go to ask for help.

Saying F**k It When You Can't Say F**k It to Being Broke

I've been broke. I know what it's like to exist on benefits, to have to sell the last things you own to pay the bills, to not be able to pay the bills, to scrape by on a low wage wondering whether you'll get through to the end of the week or month on what's in your wallet.

It's agonizing. And financial worries aren't restricted to those living from month to month on benefits or a low income. I've been a house owner and still terrified by financial anxieties and fears of bankruptcy.

Whether your financial worries are acute or chronic, regardless of what others might say about them, there is a unique quality to the pain of financial anxieties. You only know it if you've experienced it. It eats away at you day and night. And it's not a pain you can easily say F**k It to.

This is about basic survival after all. This is about sheltering yourself (and maybe your family too), about feeding and clothing yourself, heating yourself. You can't say 'Oh, F**k It, who needs to eat anyway.'

F**k It, in this case, means being able to face the situation and try to do something about it. Which is very hard to do. The classic behaviour when we start to enter financial difficulties is not to open the bills coming through the letter-box. We prefer not to know. We bury our heads in the sand. Hoping it'll all go away. But it doesn't.

The only way through is to grit your teeth, say F**k It to your huge desire to run away, and open the envelopes, and face the situation. Oh my, it's hard. I've been there, I know how hard it is.

You have to keep taking deep breaths and face it.

F∗∗**k It means being able to face the situation and try to do something about it.**

And you're probably starting to see a theme here, as we look at the things you can't say F**k It to. If F**k It usually entails getting things into perspective, and realizing that the things we're concerned about don't matter so much, and thus taking our attention off certain (not so important) things, then here we're exploring F**k It taking us in the opposite direction, so that we're recognizing how important this thing is to us, and using F**k It to make the difficult move of looking straight at it, right in the eyes.

It's not 'F**k It, it doesn't matter so much.'

It's 'F**k It, it matters, I need to pay attention to this (even though I want to run away).'

Saying F**k It When You Can't Say F**k It to Being Ill

Remember, there's no international sliding scale of suffering. This is not a competition. It's how you feel that matters. At different times in my life, I've had exactly the same symptoms create very different feelings in me. An asthma attack that had me rushed to hospital as a child, but hardly bothered me emotionally, would have me panicking and frightened now.

I've experienced illness in various forms in my life. I spent a lot of time in hospital (having been rushed there) as a child. Throughout my life, I've spent long nights unable to sleep because I'd be gasping for breath. And other nights not being able to sleep because my skin was sore and bleeding.

I've had several anaphylactic shocks: one as a young adult, after a stray peanut, when I was so close to leaving this world, with my heartbeat fading rapidly, that my consciousness went for a ride above my body, looking down at that dying body and all the panicking medics around it, before I thought *Neehhhh, it's not my time to go* and came back down, as some drug kicked in and brought my heart back to the heart-land of the living.

I know what it's like to be chronically sick, so that every night is a struggle, and every day is a struggle: to feel sick or itchy or out of breath most of the time. I know what it's like to be embarrassed by my illness. I know what it's like to have to deal not just with the physical symptoms of an illness, but the equally debilitating mental health effects of being unwell all the time, or never sleeping properly.

I know what it's like to be terrified of getting sick too. And many more of us have experienced this with the coronavirus pandemic. Particularly in the first few months of the pandemic, I tried to stay calm, but I knew that catching the virus could put me in hospital, and that this virus attacks the lungs and leaves you gasping for breath, and I remembered how familiar I am with how that can feel.

I've mentioned elsewhere about the healing I got from saying F**k It around my overall health. But what about when you're on your sick bed, when nothing is helping, when you're in pain, sometimes agony, when the prognosis isn't good, when there's no obvious cure? It's hard to say 'F**k It, it doesn't matter so much' when you can hardly breathe, or every moment brings pain.

If you're suffering financial pain, you can try to ignore those envelopes full of bills. Whereas this form of pain can't be ignored. It is relentless and constant, and there is no alternative than for it to be faced.

So this is how I use F**k It in such cases.

I've noticed a huge difference in how I responded to illness as a child, compared to how I respond to it as an adult. I was actually more ill as a child than at many of the times I've been ill as an adult. But I've struggled so much more as an adult. And it's been because of my thought process around the illness. As a child, I lived in the present, thankfully devoid of the contemplation of the future (when I might continue to be ill) or the past (when I'd been ill before). I just experienced the pain and discomfort, as painful and uncomfortable as they were, in the present. Whereas, as an adult, I'd agonize over how it would be living like this, and how it might get worse, and contemplating how I wouldn't be able to take it.

So, if I were to get sick today, I'd aim to say F**k It to all those thought processes about the future and the past. I'd aim to concentrate on today, on getting through today, and say F**k It to the rest.

AIM TO CONCENTRATE ON TODAY, ON GETTING THROUGH TODAY, AND SAY FK IT TO THE REST.**

I would still face my feelings – 'F**k It, this is how I'm feeling now' – but I'd also deploy F**k It to sort those painful thoughts: 'F**k It, I'll just get through today, then we'll see.'

Saying F**k It When You Can't Say F**k It to Being Terrified

I know what it's like to be terrified. I was taught very early in life. Very early indeed.

When I was being born, I got stuck on my way out. My shoulder got stuck, and the doctors couldn't get me out. And everyone was panicking. I guess my mum was panicking. That was my first experience of the outside world, as I emerged into it (I made it out alive, of course, in the end): panic and terror (and I guess, after that, some relief).

I've experienced a replay of this terrifying experience (of getting stuck) once or twice a year for the whole of my life. Just put me in a bedroom that's too dark at night and I'll invariably head into a nightmare of being trapped in a cave, or in a small space, or aware that I'm in a bed but not able to escape, and I'll be absolutely terrified and usually then crawl around the room for a while, and scream for help. Yeah, great.

I know terrified. I've been terrified in various situations in my life. Serious car accidents, earthquakes, emergency plane landings, erupting volcanoes, driving through forest fires, being struck by lightning, stuck lifts in disused buildings, vicious fights outside pubs, muggings, witnessing someone intentionally pushing someone else onto a live underground train line, oh, and stepping up onto a stage alone in front of 2,000 people.

It's hard to say F**k It to terrified. You can't relax and let go when you're terrified.

ACTION IS THE ANTIDOTE TO TERROR.

But you can say F**k It to everything else and ACT. Action is the antidote to terror. I've had to say, a few too many times in my life, 'Leave everything and just run'.

Action, in the face of terrifying threat, is the nervous system in fight-or-flight mode… confronting the threat, or running away.

It's likely that we're able to do it naturally. But another natural response is to freeze. And that usually doesn't help. Though sometimes you have no choice. If you do have the choice, act.

I had no choice on a scorching July day in Naples, when I was standing at a pedestrian crossing with Gaia and our two boys, hands holding onto two large suitcases, and a small bag on a strap over my shoulder containing all my documents, credit cards and phone. The lights changed so we were just starting to cross. I saw the guy on the scooter and got worried when it looked like he wasn't going to stop, then I saw he had a plastic carrier bag over his face, like a mask, and I thought '*weird*'. He weaved through the people, I was in horror for the boys' safety, but he leaned over to me and snatched at my bag, the strap of which snapped, and off he went, with my bag. It happened so quickly; I had no time to understand it before he was gone. I had no time to duck out of the way, or free my hands to defend myself and my bag, or pull him off the scooter.

He was gone and we stood there in a kind of daze as I realized what he'd just taken: my phone, and all that was on there, my passport, my drivers' licence, and all my debit and credit cards. We soon saw there was a parked police car just down the road. We rushed to them and told them what had happened. They shrugged and said that there was nothing they could do.

I'd not had time to be terrified. I'd not had time to act. My fight-or-flight response rose up as the plastic-bag-masked scooter-man scootered away. I cancelled my cards, I ordered replacements of the documents, I bought another phone and hoped that my screen had locked in time to protect all my data.

But, over the following days, a delayed shock set in.

I was dreaming about it. I was more nervous.

I shared what had happened with my therapist, who's trained in somatic experiencing, as Gaia is. And she immediately recognized that my body had activated in response to the situation, but not in time to make the action of fighting or fleeing. So she guided me in replaying the situation in my head, where I had time to see what was happening, and thus act. In this scenario I managed to pull the guy off the scooter, and, without going into detail, I was able to fully and physically act in response to his threat to me and my family. And that did it: no more dreams, no more nervousness. Though I do look out for people wearing plastic carrier bags for masks.

If you're terrified – for whatever reason – but feel you can, say F**k It and act, in whatever way you can.

Saying F**k It When You Can't Say F**k It to Pandemics

It's hard to remember life before the pandemic. We hope it's a once-in-a-lifetime experience, but they say there could be more coming. I like to say, 'I hope it's the closest any of us get to a home-front war-time experience in our lifetimes.'

In fact, I've found that, during the pandemic, there have been quite a few things along those lines that I've 'liked to say'. And I guess that's because, as we've tried to make sense of what's been going on, we grab onto things that either help us make sense of it, or somehow reassure us. I've also been saying, when asked what I think will happen, something like, 'Well, what we know so far, is that it's almost impossible to tell what will happen next, or how we'll feel, because everything keeps changing so quickly, including how we feel.'

It may be hard to wonder how you can say F**k It in the face of a global pandemic (it matters, it's a pandemic, it's making people very sick, and many are losing their lives). I've had to say it many times.

Even today, I will have to say F**k It as I don a mask to go into a shop or supermarket where no one else is bothering to wear a mask despite all the requests to do so.

In fact, this pandemic has been the perfect test of F**k It in all its forms and applications.

F**k It is about tuning in to what is right for me, no matter what everyone else is saying or doing. So I've said F**k It and walked past the hundreds of packed-out restaurants and bars down the road from where we live, and I'd insist on eating outside or getting a takeaway instead.

F**k It is about keeping things in perspective, even when the frightening details are looming large. In this pandemic, there have been so many challenges, inconveniences, set-backs and disappointments. We've been concerned for our own and our

> **F**k It is about tuning in to what is right for me, no matter what everyone else is saying or doing.**

family's health. We've had to cancel and reschedule events. But throughout, so far, we've been able to say 'we're okay, we're alive and our business is still okay and alive'.

And at some level, being grateful for the basics in our lives (i.e. being alive, making a living) has been a relief. It's made so many of us grateful for the joys of small things. We've appreciated nature more, friends and family more, the joys of great films and

TV more. Just imagine what you were worrying about before the pandemic – pah! Nonsense eh? Let's keep that perspective as we head out of this.

F**k It is about thinking for yourself, no matter what others are thinking, or guidelining. A quality of the early months of the pandemic, for me at least, was an obsession with the statistics and data. Before the pandemic, we knew in theory that life carries risk. We know that crossing a road carries a risk, so we'd be careful crossing roads. We know that lots of accidents happen at home, so we'd be mindful when climbing ladders, chopping vegetables or climbing into or out of a hot bath. But they were passing thoughts at best. Everyday caution in response to everyday and largely theoretical risks.

The pandemic changed that.

The risk of doing anything outside our front doors increased. We'd even disinfect mail coming through the front doors at one point. And the precise risk of doing anything out there was both uncertain and shifting. In the deepest lockdowns, one trip we would make out of that front door, as a family, with wheely suitcases (we didn't have a car) was to the supermarket.

So the chances of catching the virus on that trip were dependent on a variety of data and facts: how many people per 100,000 are currently infected in our city, and thus what are the chances that we bump into one of them in the enclosed supermarket; how many people are likely to be carrying the virus (either pre-symptomatic but infectious, or asymptomatic and infectious, or symptomatic but unheeding of their responsibility to self-isolate); how the virus is conveyed, whether as droplets on railings, or food packets, or airborne and thus possibly in the air of the supermarket, and if so, how long it would stay airborne; if I were to become infected, what affects the viral load, what are my chances of being hospitalized given my age, BMI and any health conditions, and so on.

So we'd wear masks and gloves, stay away from people as far as possible, sanitize our hands, and conscientiously disinfect every packet, item and lemon or courgette once we got home.

And, throughout this pandemic, no matter what the rules and guidelines have been, I've gone through that regular risk assessment for whatever we do.

F**k It is about feeling what I'm feeling, no matter what anyone else is feeling or suggesting how I should feel. There have been times when my feelings have been in synch with others', and other times when I've been either more stressed or more relaxed compared to the prevailing mood.

Fk It is about feeling what you're feeling, no matter what anyone else is feeling or suggesting you should feel.**

I think for myself. I feel for myself. And you can do the same.

F**k It is about going your own way, doing your own thing, but not when it puts others at obvious risk. I'm liberal: I think people should generally be able to go about their business as they think best, behave how they want to behave, believe what they want to believe, say what they want to say, wear want they want to wear.

But, in this pandemic, the wearing of masks and the possibility of vaccination have raised interesting questions about personal freedom versus public safety.

The wearing of masks is particularly interesting, ethically. The average mask is said to provide relatively little protection for the wearer in terms of catching the virus, but relatively high protection for others in the vicinity if the wearer is infectious but wearing a mask. So, wearing a mask is mainly for the benefit of others, though it does have some benefit for the wearer. It's also not risky for the wearer, just a little uncomfortable. So in contexts where masks are being advised or mandated for the safety of the community, to argue for the personal freedom of not wearing a mask is to place our individual freedom over the freedom of others not to be infected by us. I have a feeling masks will be with us for a while, so please say F**k It to whatever ideas you have or have heard, and, if it's recommended to do so, wear one.

The pandemic has reminded me again that we all have a right to feel how we feel. Despite the common threat, there was no common response. In one of my gloomiest moments, struggling with a full-fat lockdown and its effects on our lives and business, I was walking through the park where a group of people in their 30s were dancing to music and I overheard 'Long live lockdown and furlough, it's like one massive summer holiday.'

Breathe. We all have a right to feel how we feel.

Saying F**k It When You Can't Say F**k It to Other Ongoing Threat-to-life Issues

The ethical and political questions raised by the pandemic, in terms of individual freedom, responsibility to the community and state intervention, will become more familiar in another ongoing threat-to-life situation: climate change. This is not just a threat to individual lives, but to life on Earth full-stop.

Again, we'll have to think more about that balance between expressing our own personal freedom and any harm that that freedom might do to the climate and other humans.

It's becoming increasingly obvious that every aspect of our lives – what we eat and drink in terms of meat-eating or veggie, organic or not, local or not, and what we do with the packaging; how we get about and what cars we drive, if any; how we heat our homes; where we go on holiday; where we invest our money and pensions – has an impact on the planet and on the other humans inhabiting it.

I'm literally married to Gaia, Gaia Pollini, but we're all realizing that every one of us is married to Gaia, or the Gaia principle of the Earth: 'that living organisms interact with their inorganic surroundings on Earth to form a synergistic and self-regulating, complex system that helps to maintain and perpetuate the conditions for life on the planet'[1].

EVERY ASPECT OF OUR LIVES HAS AN IMPACT ON THE PLANET AND ON THE OTHER HUMANS INHABITING IT.

So our continued existence as humans may require another evolutionary step: hard-wiring in the awareness that survival of the planet-wide human community and the planet's biodiversity is necessary to the survival of the individual, me.

And this shifts the emphasis of F**k It too.

As much as we tune in to what we need, and reject the 'shoulds' and the 'oughts' to follow our own way, we'll increasingly need to

---

1 Wikipedia (2002), 'Gaia hypothesis': https://en.wikipedia.org/wiki/Gaia_hypothesis [Accessed 9 January 2022]

tune in to a more universal need, and reject the planet-destroying imperatives of the self-orientated, to restore a more natural way.

So as we expand our awareness from our narrow selves to our wider planet-inhabiting communities, so we'll be able to use F**k It differently. Many of us will have to say a whole range of big F**k Its in order to eat differently and more sustainably, travel differently and more sustainably, invest differently and more sustainably, to, overall, live differently and more sustainably.

As a community, as a (human) race, we're clearly going to have to say F**k It to a variety of habits and addictions, most obviously and urgently to fossil fuels, that leave us facing the various existential crises that now confront us.

Saying F**k It When You Can't Say F**k It to Death and Dying

Both the pandemic and the climate crisis have us toggling between both individual and universal fears. The existential quality to these crises is not new. The first half of the 20th century was overshadowed by the apocalyptic intensity of two world wars. For the second half of the century, the threat was nuclear apocalypse. And in the 2,000 years since the Book of Revelation mentioned the four horsemen of the apocalypse in the Bible, the fear of apocalypse would likely have been experienced by most humans and stoked by plague, pestilence, famine and war.

So, though the new awareness of burning, flooding and choking ourselves out of existence feels new, it's not.

And neither is the awareness that we, and our loved ones, are going to die, of course. Maybe a significant element that sets us apart from other animals is our full consciousness of our own mortality.

But, though we humans have been aware of our mortality since we became conscious, we don't seem to be getting any better at dealing with it. No, we can't easily say F**k It to death and dying.

There are cultures and religions, of course, that have a go at softening the blow. They tend to introduce the idea that life doesn't actually end, but goes on in a different format. That format might be as a reincarnated being, or in some kind of idyllic afterlife, when suffering ends, or as an ongoing spirit form.

It's not just a continuation of life that is imagined, but a much-improved version of it. If you hold such a concept, and it comforts you, bless you (and I'm not assuming that you've just sneezed, more offering you the kind of comforting words that you're likely to be familiar with).

THOUGH WE HAVE BEEN AWARE OF OUR MORTALITY SINCE WE BECAME CONSCIOUS, WE DON'T SEEM TO BE GETTING ANY BETTER AT DEALING WITH IT.

For the rest of us, and that's probably an increasing number of people on the planet if you take into account movements away from organized religion and growing populations, the end is the end. In fact, there are probably more humans on the planet who think that the end is the end than ever before in human history.

I prefer to flip 'Pascal's wager'.

Blaise Pascal was a 17th-century French philosopher who argued that a rational person would believe in God, and live accordingly, because to do so would have (literally) infinite rewards, against the finite losses (of earthly pleasures presumably), whereas a non-believer might enjoy those finite earthly pleasures, but suffer infinite losses (i.e. in 'hell', though that too presumed some belief in the afterlife concept, clearly).

The issue with assuming that there's a wonderful 'after-life' awaiting us is that we don't fully appreciate the tangibly wonderful 'this-life'. It's the knowledge that the day's going to end that makes the appreciation of the day deeper and sweeter.

Anyway, most of us don't have the option of hedging our bets on any particular belief system to suit our finite or infinite needs. Through a combination of rational scientific knowledge and common sense, many of us these days are not off with the fairies, angels, gods and spirits, but down here with the living and the dying.

Which takes us back to our original issue. If we can't say F**k It (it doesn't really matter) to death and dying, then what do we do about all that pain?

Because it is inherently painful. The thought that we're going to decay and die is so painful that we try not to think about it. The thought that our loved ones are going to decay and die is likely to be even more painful.

But think about it we should.

Saying F**k It in this context is not to lighten it, or soften it, it's to think about it.

Or rather, to *feel* about it.

If death and dying are currently not a significant part of your life, do think and feel about it occasionally. Feel the pain of loss.

Because it's likely that the pain of loss, and the fear of loss, do pervade your life anyway. Maybe it's the loss of your youth, or your job, or your looks, or your status, or a relationship, or your local department store, that you fear, but underneath that fear of that loss is likely to be the fear of the ultimate loss: death and dying.

And if death and dying are part of your life: if you're losing someone dear, or have lost someone dear, or are very sick yourself, I'm sorry. Breathe. I have some experience of knowing how difficult dealing with death can be. Of what agony it can be. Of thinking that you'll never feel okay again. That the intensity of loss will never go away. Your experience will be unique to you, but I do have some experience of the pain of it.

And, in the pain, we need to do what we need to do. F**k It in this case is to follow the requirement of the pain and grief. To not be diverted from its requirement by anyone else's requirements of you. It's to cry when you need to cry. To say what you need to say to others. To feel it as much as you need to feel it. To distract and divert when you need to distract and divert.

F**k It is, at the core level, always the same; it's to follow the natural way, no matter what others might say or do, or what they believe you should do or say.

Do follow the natural way when you face death and dying – it's a painful and agonizing way, but, when most of us know the end is the end, when we're going to lose these people from our lives for what we know as 'forever', or they're going to lose us for what

F****k It is, at the core level, always the same; it's to follow the natural way.**

they know as 'forever', then that being about the most painful thing that could be is also about the most natural thing that could be.

And we might also see that it's a most beautiful thing, too, as the pain arises from this most intense appreciation, both of the people we love and of the true nature of our finite time on this Earth and the finite beings that inhabit it. There's a sweetness of sadness to this that we miss if we look through the refracted lens of the infinite.

PART 5

THE EFFECT OF SAYING F**K IT

F**k It, I Just Love Being Alive NOW

Sure, in the summer in which I'm writing this, there's a still raging pandemic, climate change is burning California and flooding Germany, Afghanistan is falling apart, populations are split down the middle politically and by the so-called 'culture wars', and there are a hundred other reasons to support the thesis that NOW is a very rubbish time to be alive.

But, I'm sorry, F**k It, I am quite happy to be alive right now. This very day, I noticed that a new symbol had appeared on the Google bar on my phone – a camera. And a few moments later, I was pointing my camera at everything and learning and laughing and beginning to glimpse the huge possibility of this.

I know, I know, it's old hat by the time you read this. But I'm excited, super-excited – I'm even excited by the fact that we

Brits are increasingly using 'super' as an adjective instead of 'very'. Another American import that's super-easy to adopt.

Though, also this morning, I read that American toddlers are speaking with an English accent because all they've been watching during long lockdown hours at home is *Peppa Pig*. So there are kids in Ohio saying, 'Pray, mother, would you care for a cup of tea?'

I was super-thrilled to read this because it shows the traffic is not just one-way.

In fact, EVEN with a still-raging pandemic, I'm glad to be alive now – because we have such brilliant scientists able to develop vaccines in record-quick-times and bring new treatments onstream.

So whenever you're getting gloomy because of whatever's grimming you out about life in these times, say F**k It and realize how lucky we are to be alive NOW.

Not that we have any choice anyway.

Life responds when you say F**k It to it

You've taken your two kids out for a Chinese meal. Flynn is five and Lizzie is seven. You're tired. The crispy duck is taking a while to arrive and the kids are getting restless. Flynn unfolds the starched serviette, puts it on his head and starts making 'Ooohhhh, oooohhh' noises, as if he's a ghost. Lizzie joins in before you've had a chance to utter a word.

The 'oohhhhhhs' rapidly rise in volume and you ask the kids to stop it: 'We're in a restaurant and you'll disturb other people.' In fact, those other people are already starting to get disturbed and are looking round.

Your initial pleas have no effect, and you now have several courses of action open to you:

1. You get heavy and use whatever methods you normally employ to control your children (these could range from bribery, such as 'You won't get an ice cream', to the creation of fear, such as 'You wait until I get you home' or 'I'll tell your dad about this').

2. You don't get heavy at all, but get increasingly frustrated that your kids aren't listening to you – this usually ends in some outburst on your part.

3. You give in and just go with it.

No. 1 works if your methods are good enough, or if you're scary enough. Well, it may work on this occasion. But kids are kids, and unless you make them very, very scared of you, they will constantly resist your attempts to control them.

No. 2 involves no serious attempt to control your kids, but no acceptance of them either. This is a hopeless place to be in and is the cause of the most stress.

No. 3 is the hardest and riskiest to do because it goes against everything that parents are told about discipline and boundaries.

But imagine this: you put your own serviette on your head and start 'ooohhhing' too. The kids love it and 'oohhh' back for a while. But you know what happens? They soon get bored and move on to something else that is – usually – quieter and less disruptive for other people. And those other people soon forget that they've been disturbed in the first place.

Child-rearing discourses aside, let's look at a child as a metaphor for life.

Most of us – as we've discussed – try to control our lives to the smallest detail. We have very sophisticated methods for controlling life, in fact, just like the parent who used method No. 1.

You might well see some of these methods in action in your parents. Parents are past masters at the trying-to-control-life game. Parents – usually with the aid of more monetary resources than they had when they were younger – try to eliminate all forms of discomfort from their lives.

They set up comfortable routines, fill their houses with comforting ornaments and rugs to put on toilet seats, and talk about things that threaten no one, such as the best route to Cirencester or how to put up sheds. They eat comforting foods (creamy things, baked things, roasted things) and watch comforting television (like shows about baking).

But as their methods get more and more sophisticated/desperate, life seems to mess around with their plans to an even greater extent. The house gets broken into, pipes burst, they get ill and people start dying all over the place.

The controlled and 'comfortable' life is not the path of wisdom or happiness, I'm afraid. But neither is the half-baked attempt to control life with method No. 2.

No. 2 is a shit way to live. At least the controller has some vim, some direction. When you're trying to control but not quite sure, you're just knocked around on the stormy sea of life. You're pissed off, but can't quite be bothered enough to get up to do something about it.

This is the path to misery.

When we give in to life – when we say F**k It at any level – we begin to ride on the wave of life. When you stick the serviette on your own head, a few things happen:

* You actually enjoy yourself, because the game is a good one and you've stopped resisting it.

* The kids love you for it and may even remember this for the rest of their lives – without the normal parental resistance to what they're doing, they usually stop what they're doing much sooner than you'd expect.

So, I'm sorry to be shoving you in and out of metaphors, especially when they're close to home… but the same thing happens with life. When you give in to life, the same things happen:

* You start enjoying yourself, because the game of life is a good one and you've stopped resisting it.

* Life seems to love it when you stop resisting, and starts coming your way more.

* Life ebbs and flows very naturally of its own accord. If you hit something nasty, it's soon replaced naturally by something lovely.

Of course, the second statement is the one that you might be wondering about the most. This is counter-intuitive. We're taught that, to get anything in life, we have to work hard and strive for it. We have to set goals and work towards them. We have to work out what matters to us and we need to ruthlessly put those things first and try to nurture them. We believe that if we don't really strive for things, then we won't get them. But, possibly, the opposite is true.

If we find the courage to loosen our hold on things… to stop wanting things so much… to stop working so hard and striving so much… to give up some of the things that matter to us… something magical happens:

We naturally start getting what we originally wanted, but without the effort

Now this is very zen and potentially very confusing: to get what you want you must give up wanting it.

But look at it like this: any form of desire and striving involves some form of tension. When you let go of the desire, the tension goes. And the relaxation that replaces it tends to attract good things into your life.

Back to the child metaphor: when you give up wanting so much for your child – wanting them to be top of the class, the best at sport, go to the best university and get the best job – when you truly give up these desires and you just sit back and let your child be, the child feels absolute freedom.

SAY FK IT AND LIFE WILL BE SO GRATEFUL IT WILL SHOWER YOU WITH BLESSINGS.**

And, funnily enough, with their sense of freedom they tend to excel at whatever they turn their attention to. So you get what you wanted precisely through *not* wanting it. When you give up wanting everything to be just so – when you say F**k It – life will be so grateful it will shower you with blessings.

The Effect on Your Mind of Saying F**k It

You notice the beauty in unexpected things

Have you ever watched a young child playing? Or can you remember what was going on inside your head as a child? I've done both – the first when my boys were young, and the second when I really relax, because I remember then what it was like to be a child.

If I lie down and look up into a blue sky and listen to the sound of a distant aeroplane, it invariably brings up a memory from my childhood. Why? Because as we grow up, we stop being fascinated by ordinary things. So when I do occasionally take pleasure simply in what's around me, it reminds me of the last time I did that: when I was a child.

This is what children do. They live in the miracle of existence. Everything is new and fascinating. They can enjoy the wrapping as much as the present… a leaking tap as much as a beautiful lake… the smell of rain falling on dry concrete as much as the smell of baking bread.

CHILDREN LIVE IN THE MIRACLE OF EXISTENCE.

There are no rules about what's good or bad, what's better than something else, or what's worth it. There's little discernment: there are just things coming in… and most of them are fascinating.

As we grow up we learn how to discern, discriminate and filter out. And we tend to filter out the ordinary things in favour of the extraordinary and the unusual. In fact, much of the time we're so lost in thoughts of the past or worries about the future that we don't have much time for any kind of appreciation. But when we do, it tends to be the things that adults think are worth appreciating: tasty things, beautiful things, interesting things and expensive things.

At some point the feeling of wooden boards under our feet, the sound of a toilet flushing in a room upstairs, the feeling of wind against our face... these all disappear off the list of things that we should appreciate. Instead we spend lots of money to go on holiday, or go to the theatre or go out for a meal in order to flex our appreciation muscles.

When we say F**k It to anything, the meanings start to crumble. As the things that matter lose their meaning, suddenly the world opens up again. Without the discrimination and discernment we learned as we were growing up, every single thing has the potential to be appreciated. Everything is beautiful.

If this happens all of a sudden it can be mind-blowing (almost literally).

And this is what happens to a lot of people who have apparently 'awakened'. When you start seeing the beauty in absurd things, you know you're starting to lose your mind. Or at least the mind that's learned to see meaning in only a limited range of things.

See each moment as having infinite potential for beauty. We tend to drag all our judgements, conditioning and boundaries from the past into the present. And it squashes that moment into something very limited. If you leave some of those judgements behind and just see things as a young child might see them, you start to get a beautiful feeling. It's a feeling of relief, but mixed with some kind of longing, too. The

> **SEE EACH MOMENT AS HAVING INFINITE POTENTIAL FOR BEAUTY.**

longing rises up from a very deep part of you that remembers what it was like to see things like this all the time.

When we say F**k It we turn the clock back. We unlearn meaning and smash the things that we've come to think mattered. We regress to a more natural state where things don't mean much but they're all just so bloody beautiful.

Anxiety evaporates over time

When anything that matters goes pear-shaped you feel anxious and stressed. In fact, simply the possibility of the things that matter going pear-shaped makes you feel anxious and stressed.

Given the vast range of things that matter to us, there's a hell of a lot of potential for anxiety. And anxiety and stress will make you ill over time. So it's worth trying to give them up and using the patches instead.

When you begin to say F**k It to things, the anxiety vanishes. Late for work and stressed about it? Say F**k It and the stress disappears immediately.

The more you say F**k It, the more you'll realize that most things don't matter that much really. And your anxiety, over time, will evaporate.

Sure, you'll still get anxious around some things, but that's life. And anxiety in the right context can be a useful response. If you're driving your car down a country road and you round a corner to find an elephant hurtling towards you, it's helpful to feel a tad anxious. Your adrenaline will start to pump, giving you all sorts of special powers that will help you deal effectively with the imminent elephant threat.

If the adrenaline isn't enough, and the only scenario is a good squashing by said elephant, then, by all means, say F**k It before you go.

It may make your ride to heaven a little easier. This is, of course, belief-dependent, as the very use of the word 'fuck' might send you to hell in some belief systems.

Your views change and become less rigid

I've always felt a little sorry for politicians. Well, someone has to, don't they? They have to work out what they believe on every issue under the sun – which is hard enough in itself – and they then have to stick to it for the rest of their lives.

There's room for a tiny bit of manoeuvre, of course, over a whole political lifetime. But very little. And rethinking is slammed as a 'U-turn'.

Now, as long as I'm not putting other cars at risk, I'm all in favour of the U-turn. If you realize you've been going the wrong way, it's much better to slam on the brakes and screech round onto the other carriageway like they do in American movies.

You never hear politicians say: 'Look, I've actually sat down and thought about this properly, and I realize I've been a complete arse. I now think precisely the opposite to before. Sorry.'

Along with our relentless accumulation of meaning, we accumulate views on everything. And these tend to become more fixed as we get older. Of course, views come in every shape and size, but they're still views.

You may have views on big subjects: that no one should be allowed to starve, that persecution should not be tolerated, that nuclear powers should be disarmed. You may have views on small subjects: that Sue down the road should kick out Mick after that fling he had with Mandy, that the chip shop on the corner should bring back the battered and deep-fried Mars Bars, that your neighbour should repaint their fence so it's not the colour of a Mars Bar.

But they're all still views. And all views are related to something that matters. When you start to say F**k It and things begin to matter less, then you start to lose your love of views. Ultimately, if nothing mattered at all then you'd have no views at all. You'd have no position, no stance, no argument. You'd just react to things as they happened: completely freshly.

In the process of things mattering less, your views may change. They'll certainly become less rigid.

People who start to say F**k It turn from vegetarians to meat-eaters, from activists in a cause to passivists, from pacifists to apathists. And if I've made up a few words there for the sake of a point and a rhythm, hey, F**k It.

I once held the view that English should be written correctly. That you shouldn't start a sentence with 'and' or 'but', for example. But one day I said F**k It. And now I'm starting every other sentence with such conjunctions, I'm using fucking fuck every other word, and I'm making up newly fancivist words.

THESE DAYS, MY ONLY REAL VIEW IS OUT OF MY EYES, IN THIS MOMENT.

I once had a prepared view on everything. This is a sad confession, but when politicians were asked questions on the radio or TV, I'd imagine how I'd answer. These days, my only real view is out of my eyes, in this moment.

You lose the plot

No, I don't mean you'll go potty. Although of course you might – and even if you don't, it may appear to people around you that you have.

This is what I mean by losing the plot. Let's say your life is a film. The 'plot' of your life is something you've pretty well figured out at the moment (well, you think so anyway):

★ You have a good idea about how the main character (i.e. you) will act in given circumstances.

★ You know what's gone before and you pretty much understand it.

★ You recognize, and understand, the setting of each scene.

★ You have pretty good ideas about what should happen in the rest of the play/film.

★ You have a very clear sense of a beginning, a middle and an end.

When you start to say F**k It to things, everything softens and blurs. The film suddenly starts to look more like a French movie from the 1960s. Your French has gone, though, so you can't understand the dialogue, and the subtitles are slightly too small from where you're sitting.

More specifically, this is what happens:

★ Given the rules that the main character (i.e. you) acts by are crumbling, it gets less and less easy to see what you will do in any given circumstance.

★ The meaning of what has happened to you becomes less clear and your past somehow seems less solid.

★ The setting of each scene suddenly becomes vast and full of possibilities, whereas before you were only seeing what you wanted to see.

★ You plan less and less; you may lose a sense of purpose and you see that your life could go in any (infinite) number of directions.

★ Your perception of time shifts and you realize that there is only really a middle: a present moment of existence.

The Effect on Your Body of Saying F**k It

The body softens

If we have a tense thought, that tension is also represented in the body. So if you release a tense thought by saying F**k It, you begin to release the tension in your body.

Just have a go with one thing now. Pick something that you're anxious about today. You probably don't have to look very far. Take a big inbreath and think about that thing and how anxious it makes you feel. Then, as you breathe out, say F**k It and feel the release in your body. Do this again.

If this can happen with one thing in your life, imagine what would happen if you could do it to a whole range of things.

When you really start to say F**k It in your life, your whole body will begin to soften. You may not notice it at first, but it will certainly start to happen. In fact, other people might notice it before you do. Your face will soften, so people may remark

SAY FK IT AND FEEL THE RELEASE IN YOUR BODY.**

that you look younger. Your neck and shoulders will soften, so you may stop having those headaches, or aches and pains in those areas. All your muscles will soften and feel heavier.

As your body softens you'll catch yourself just sitting and enjoying the feelings in your body. And one of those feelings will be *chi*.

Your chi flows

The more you say F**k It and the more you relax, the more your *chi* will flow.

Chi, remember, is the life-force that flows through you. You'll feel it as a tingling or a warmth or a magnetic feeling.

If you don't know what it feels like, it's time to learn how to play the energy accordion. So don your energetic beret, eat some energy garlic and pick up an imaginary accordion.

Now, this accordion really enjoys being played slowly – very slowly. So your hands are apart, holding the accordion. And now you start to bring your hands closer together. Don't let them touch. Just bring them slowly together. When they are very close together, start to pull the accordion open again. And continue this process. Close your eyes and focus on what you're feeling in and between your hands.

The main thing here is to relax. Relax your shoulders, relax your hands. If you don't get it today, give it a rest; you'll get it tomorrow.

But what you'll begin to feel – today or tomorrow – is *chi*.

And this stuff is the key to your health.

I love working with *chi* because it has the simplest principle: the more you relax, the more you can feel. It's not necessary to learn complicated techniques, or go from beginner classes to intermediate, then advanced, classes. No, just know that the more you relax, the more you'll feel.

So when you say F**k It to anything, because you're releasing tension in the body, more *chi* will be flowing.

THE MORE YOU RELAX, THE MORE YOU CAN FEEL.

Your body will rebalance itself

Any tension in the body creates an energy imbalance.

In Traditional Chinese Medicine, all the meridians that flow around the body are related to different energetic organ systems. If you create physical tension in any of these areas, you create a block to the energy flow that has an effect on that organ system.

Imagine how you are at work. You may well be hunched over a computer all day, worrying about this or that. The hunching alone creates tension in your shoulders, neck and back, and the worried thoughts on top of this simply add to the tension. And you can sit like that for hours.

All that tension is blocking the vital flow of energy around the body, and you begin to get imbalances. An energetic imbalance can start to affect how you are – your emotions and feelings – and it can also begin to affect your health.

Whenever you say F**k It and relax into something you were previously tense around, the energy will begin to flow through what was previously blocked. Your energy system will begin to rebalance itself.

Illnesses will disappear

Given that the idea is that many illnesses are created by these energy imbalances, any rebalancing can lead to the releasing of illness.

This is what happens when you have acupuncture. The needles are placed in points where energy blocks are occurring and – wham bam – the energy starts to flow again.

If you relax enough, you get the same effect.

Every time you say F**k It to something, it can be like one well-placed needle in your body. So you will begin to feel better. You'll feel like you have more energy (and we're talking about the traditional stuff this time, not *chi* energy). You may need less sleep and less food. And illnesses can begin to subside and heal (just look what happened to me).

You will live longer

The effect of all this relaxing is, ultimately, to significantly raise the chances of increasing the length of your life (horrible life-shortening accidents aside, of course).

If you say F**k It to one big area of tension in your life, you're likely to increase the amount of time you spend on this Earth.

Whenever you relax fully you slow down the process of ageing.

So, funnily enough, the less life means to you, the more of it you get.

THE LESS LIFE MEANS TO YOU, THE MORE OF IT YOU GET.

PART 6

THE F**K IT FORM

Saying F**k It is enough to sort anyone out (it is, after all, the Ultimate Spiritual Way). Relaxing deeply and letting go can resolve just about any problem. The simple act of relaxing is more powerful than any form of yoga or Tai Chi. The truth is, though, that our minds like a bit of form: something to get stuck into, to learn and remind us that we're doing ourselves good. So welcome to The F**k It Form. The form without form.

The F**k It Form takes postures from life (such as being slumped on the sofa watching TV), adjusts them slightly, adds a dash of consciousness (awareness of what you're doing) and a dollop-full of relaxation, and gives you a great form that will do you a lot of good. Indeed, the precise benefits of each posture are given here, so you've plenty to chew on.

The Roots of the F**k It Form

The F**k It Form is a form of Chi Kung. Just like Tai Chi is a form of Chi Kung. Let me explain. Chi Kung is the Chinese energy practice. In fact, it literally means 'practice with energy'. And this means that any time you consciously work with your energy, you are doing Chi Kung. If you sit there now, reading this book, and relax your body and imagine the *chi* flowing through your hands, then you are doing Chi Kung.

That's what I love about it.

You don't have to go to classes, you don't have to read any books, you don't have to learn any complicated forms, you can just do Chi Kung wherever you are.

I mean, you can do all those other things if you want. I went to classes for years, read dozens of books, learned many complicated forms, so help yourself if that's what you fancy. But you won't get anywhere any faster by doing those things. In fact, I guarantee that you'll experience more energy sooner doing The F**k It Form than by learning Tai Chi.

And, yes, Tai Chi is a form of Chi Kung, too. It's probably the most famous form. It is a typical Chi Kung moving form: the movements are very slow, and they are designed to exercise different energy systems of the body. The problem, though, with a form like Tai Chi, is that it takes such a very long time to learn properly. It can take a couple of years to learn the basic moves. And that's before you start to learn the deep energetic work. I love Tai Chi, and I'm glad I put in the hours, because I don't think I could be bothered nowadays.

THE F**K IT FORM: EXPEND LITTLE EFFORT AND GET MAXIMUM RESULTS.

The F**k It Form is for those who want to feel the benefits of Chi Kung, but without the effort. And – by the way –

that is very much the Taoist way: to expend little effort and get maximum results.

So here's the form that requires the least effort: the form that says F**k It to Form. Like Tai Chi, if you do the whole form you'll give your whole energy system a thorough cleansing.

If you do this form every day for a month, you'll notice profound benefits: you'll feel noticeably more relaxed, all of the time, you'll sleep better, your appetite will stabilize, and you'll begin to heal any illness.

Like anything of a F**k It nature, don't take it too seriously, and don't attach yourself to any of these predicted benefits. Do it because you like the feeling of energy in your body, and because you're one of the first to practise a new world-wide energetic form.

Practice

The whole idea of the F**k It Form is that you can do it as part of your normal day. Each position is based on something that you already do. So all you have to do is make a tiny adjustment to your position (such as making sure your feet are parallel, or your knees are slightly bent), breathe consciously and become aware of your chi, and – hey presto – you're doing The F**k It Form.

So daily practice is important if you want to start building up your *chi*. If you can't even manage a little practice in a day, you lazy dog, then say F**k It and just try it tomorrow.

Breathing

Breathing is vital for all the postures and movements. Otherwise you'll die. And we don't want any deaths, do we now?

It's worth starting to play with belly-breathing in the F**k It Form. Belly-breathing? Yes, breathing into your belly, old chap. If you watch a baby breathing, you'll notice that the first thing that happens when they breathe in is that their belly inflates. And as they breathe out, their belly deflates. This is the natural way of breathing.

For one reason or another, at some point in our childhood (probably when we get very scared about something) we begin to breathe mainly into our chests. So if you observe most adults breathing, their chests will rise as they breathe in and fall as they breathe out. And not a lot will be happening in their bellies. This way of breathing can be very good for emergencies, but it isn't so good for normal life. It's a shallow breath – and shallow breath means shallow life.

If you want to live more deeply, you have to breathe more deeply. And that means getting the breath down into your belly (or that's what it feels like anyway because of the movement of your diaphragm. In reality, your lungs are not extending down into your belly!). So try it now: as you breathe in, push out the muscles of your belly. Imagine there's a balloon in your belly and you have to inflate the balloon with each inbreath. And then deflate the balloon with each outbreath.

IF YOU WANT TO LIVE MORE DEEPLY, YOU HAVE TO BREATHE MORE DEEPLY.

Just learning how to breathe like this can change your life. Just changing from a chest (shallow) breather to a belly (deep) breather can have tremendous physiological effects. You're filling your lungs more effectively (with a chest breath you'll never fill more than two-thirds of your lungs), so you're getting more oxygen (the main fuel for your body).

The new action of your diaphragm (it pushes down deeply on the inbreath rather than lifting up slightly) creates a tremendous massage for all your internal organs. The massaged organs get a rush of blood, which is as welcome as a warm shower. The whole intestinal system gets a good massage, too, allowing it to give your body what it needs more effectively and get rid of the stuff that it doesn't.

The other great thing about belly-breathing is that you have to discard some vanity (shallow), as with really good belly-breathing your belly will puff out to the size of Buddha's (and he had a great belly). You can replace some of this vanity with acceptance (deep), and enjoy the feeling of health and relaxation that this breathing brings.

You may also need to discard belts that have fixed positions in favour of something more elastic, so everything can move more fluidly down there.

How *chi* develops

The more you consciously work with your *chi*, the more *chi* will develop in your body. Imagine that every day of conscious practice with *chi* is like putting a pound coin into a jar. Over time it really builds up. Only this jar is managed by one hell of an investment manager. At the moment he's managing to get a 200 per cent return on your investment. And, given that you're reinvesting all the profit and the holdings are giving you an extra yearly dividend, you're doing rather well. Just imagine how rich you'll be after just a few years. That's how *chi* works.

THE MORE YOU CONSCIOUSLY WORK WITH YOUR *CHI*, THE MORE *CHI* WILL DEVELOP IN YOUR BODY.

And this is how *chi* works in the moment. The Chinese say: 'First the mind. Then the *chi*. Then the blood.' (Only they say it in Chinese because it would be weird otherwise.) It's succinct but true.

When you think about a part of your body – the palm of your hand, for example – then *chi* will begin to flow there. And once the *chi* starts to flow, then blood will follow it.

That's why *chi* practice (Chi Kung) is so powerful: you get all the benefits of balancing the energy system and you get the accompanying physical benefits of blood flow, too.

So let's explore the F**k It Form:

Reclined Sitting Postures

Holding the goose's egg

To get into this basic sofa posture, slump on the sofa as if you're watching the TV. In fact, watch the TV if you want. Make sure your feet are flat on the floor, your feet are shoulder-width apart (that is, the outside of your feet should be the same distance apart as from the edge of one shoulder to the other), your spine relaxed and your head facing forwards (not up). Relax your

jaw and place the tip of your tongue on the roof of your mouth, just behind the upper teeth.

Now place your hands on your belly, one over the other. If you're a man, you should place the left hand against your belly first, then place the right hand relaxedly on top of it. If you're a woman, place the right hand against the belly first. The bottom hand should be positioned so that the base of the thumb rests comfortably against the belly button.

Now breathe slowly into this position. Start to feel the *chi* circulating.

The benefits of this posture

In this posture you're directing *chi* into the *dan tien*, the primary energy storage point in the body. This creates a general tonic for the body and is the base exercise that all other F**k It Form exercises should be built upon. If you're going to do only one exercise, then do this one. It nourishes the kidneys, so it'll help calm you down and reduce anxiety.

Peacock fans its wings

Get into the basic sofa posture (as before). Now clasp your hands behind your head, placing your thumbs just beneath the occiput (the bony ridge at the bottom of the skull). Use your thumbs to massage this area. Now breathe slowly into this position. Start to feel the *chi* circulating.

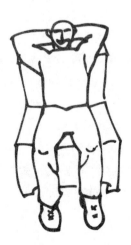

The benefits of this posture

The stretching of the arms tonifies the heart meridian – so you will feel happier within just the first minute. Pushing back the shoulders also opens your lungs, promoting deeper breathing and the releasing of any stagnant *chi*. Massaging the occiput stimulates the acupuncture point *Fengchi* – great for reducing symptoms of stress, including headaches and eye problems.

Holding the sacred bow

Get into the basic sofa posture (as before). Cross your left leg over the right, so that the left ankle rests gently on the top of the thigh of the right leg. Now grasp the ankle of the left leg with your right hand. Let your left hand simply fall onto the cushion beside you, palm facing upwards. Now breathe slowly into this position. Start to feel the *chi* circulating. When you have felt the full benefits of this position, change legs.

The benefits of this posture

The gentle stretch shifts stagnant energy in the legs, so it's a good tonic for restless, tired legs. The gallbladder meridian and yin channels of the legs are stretched, affecting your clarity and creativity. So if you want clarity in any situation – or to get an idea for something – get into this posture. Pulling the ankle further up towards the groin will increase the benefits.

Slain by dragon fire

Get into the basic sofa posture (as before). Now simply let your arms drop to your sides, palms facing up. Imagine that you have indeed been slain by a dragon, and that you're now lying lifeless in the position in which you were slain. Feel the weight of your lifeless body on the sofa. It's a great position with which to end the first sequence, just as death is a good way to end the sequence of life.

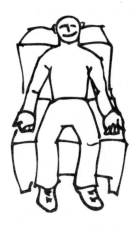

Imagine now that the dragon is still there and still breathing fire on you. Imagine that the fire is very precisely directed. First, the dragon is directing the fire at your heart. Feel the heat and the power entering your heart. The dragon then directs the fire into your solar plexus. Feel the heat and power entering this tender point. And last, the dragon directs fire into your belly, your *dan tien*. Feel the heat and power entering your *dan tien*, the primary energy centre of your whole being.

The benefits of this posture

The initial posture allows the *chi* to sink in your body. This will make you feel more grounded. You'll feel instantly calmer, less fearful and be ready to embrace life, not be scared of it.

The fire of the dragon is a very powerful healing technique. The energy enters your body and goes to wherever it is needed, as well as the point it entered. So your heart will benefit (joy), your solar plexus will benefit (openness) and your *dan tien* will benefit (centredness and energy). Then the energy moves to any area of energy imbalance in your body.

In Chinese Medicine these three areas relate to the Triple Burner – which you need to clear to create a balanced flow of energy through the body. As you do the exercise you may well start to feel a spiralling of energy down through your body.

Upright Sitting Postures

Golden hands

Get into the basic sitting posture: sit in any chair where your back can be upright and your feet can rest flat on the floor. Make sure your feet are a few inches apart and that they are parallel to each other (i.e. so that your feet are neither toe-out nor toe-in). Feel that you're sitting comfortably on your sitting bones, without any support from the back of the chair. Imagine a golden thread attached to the crown of your head that lifts your head up and straightens the spine. The pulling golden thread will also have the effect of dropping your chin slightly.

Be aware that there are two directional forces at work in your body. Imagine a coat-hanger on a rail. And on the coat-hanger hangs a silk dress. Your skeleton is the coat-hanger. And just as the coat-hanger is being suspended by the hook on the rail (an upward force), you're being suspended by the golden thread (an upward force).

Everything else in your body can be like the silk dress – just hanging from the solid support of the coat-hanger (a downward force). So all your muscles, skin, organs, the whole gooey lot of you can simply sink towards the ground (a downward force). Really feel the sensation of letting yourself sink towards the ground. Last, place the tip of your tongue lightly on the roof of your mouth, just behind the upper teeth.

That's the sitting posture. You now simply do different things with your hands.

For golden hands, let your arms just dangle by your sides. So from your shoulders down, there should be no intervention from your muscles whatsoever. Now breathe slowly into this position. And begin to feel the *chi* collecting in your hands. This is the gold of *chi* being generated: thus, golden hands.

The benefits of this posture

Lengthening the spine like this opens up the governing *du* channel, helping us stay alert and full of energy. The rising *chi* invigorates the whole body, whilst the mind calms down.

You'll feel the strong *chi* collecting in your hands and this will also boost your circulation.

You can also increase the benefit to your kidneys by rubbing your *chi*-full hands on your kidneys before you move on to the next posture.

Monkey scratches back

Get into the sitting posture (as before). With your left hand resting in your lap, take your right hand over your right shoulder, as if you're going to scratch your back. In fact, you can begin to rub your back with your fingers. Make sure that you rub either side of the spine: maybe with your first finger on one side of the spine and your index finger on the other side.

Relax and breathe into this position. You can either continue to rub the spine or just rest your hand on your back. Once you can feel the *chi* flowing and you're ready to move on, simply do the same with your left hand.

The benefits of this posture

This position stretches the heart meridian, settles your mind and allows you to massage the bladder meridian. This ultimately supports the vital kidney energy system, and helps strengthen the whole of your back. Not bad for a little rub.

Tiger's paws

Get into the sitting posture (as before). Now simply let your hands rest in your lap with the palms facing upwards. Make sure your arms are completely relaxed. Just let your hands rest there. Breathe slowly into this posture. You'll begin to feel *chi* flowing into the palms of your hands, making them feel tingly, soft and tender, like the soft paws of a tiger.

The benefits of this posture

You can sit in this posture for a long time. It is a great meditation position. Your mind will calm down and stressful thoughts will disappear. The focus on the breath strengthens the lungs and boosts *chi* in the whole body. The focus on the palms stimulates the crucial point *Laogong*. You can even try breathing through your palms: sucking in *chi* on the inbreath through these *chi* gateways, and releasing stagnant *chi* on the outbreath. Or if you prefer to keep it simple, sit there quietly and you'll notice your cold hands become warm.

Standing Postures

The resting warrior

All these standing postures are great to do when you're waiting for something. Whether it's a Tube train or a bus, or for your mate to turn up at the pub, these are perfect to get into any time you're standing around.

So, first get into the basic standing posture. Your feet should be shoulder-width apart – that is, the outside edges of your feet should be the same distance apart as your shoulders. Make sure your feet are parallel to each other, neither toe-out nor toe-in. If you want to be very precise about this, if you drew a line from the middle (the bi-section) of your heel under your foot to the middle (the bi-section) of your toes, then these are the lines that you want to be getting parallel.

Your knees should be slightly bent. The more you bend your knees, the more *chi* you'll generate, but the more difficult it is to stand for a while. So, at first, just bend your knees slightly.

Next, you need to 'tuck your tail in'. To get the feeling of what this means, stick your bum out, then do the opposite: push your bum in. This is tucking your tail in. It feels weird at first, but like the whole posture, you'll get used to it after a bit. Standing like this, with your tail tucked in, feels like perching on the edge of a bar stool. The physical effect of standing like this, with your tail tucked in, is to straighten your spine and allow the full belly-breathing to work.

Up we go now to the head, where you want to imagine the golden thread suspending your head from the crown. This will allow you to relax and drop your jaw slightly. Last, allow the tip of your tongue to lightly touch the roof of your mouth, just behind your upper teeth.

Although this may seem like a rather complicated and weird routine to go through just to stand up, you'll get the hang of it very quickly, and each pointer has a very important reason for it (which I won't go into for now at the risk of you thinking it's even more complicated than you do already). You just have to trust me on this one.

Standing like this, you're practically in the resting warrior. All you have to do now is put your hands in your trouser pockets. If you don't have any pockets, pretend you have and just rest your palms against your body.

Now just rest in this posture. Breathe slowly and deeply. And – given this posture will feel pretty peculiar – just keep bringing your attention to the bits of you that start to feel uncomfortable and simply relax them. The main thing with a posture like this – at the beginning – is to keep going… just keep relaxing. I hope the Tube or the bus or your mate take a few more minutes, because it's really good to stand like this for a while to get to feel the relaxation that comes from going through tension again and again.

The benefits of this posture

This posture – like all the standing postures – provides a great general tonic to the energy system. That's why they're at the heart of most Chi Kung practices. After just a short amount of practice you'll feel deeply calm in a way that can last for the day (or at least the Tube/bus journey or time with your mate).

Warming the heavenly globe

Get into the standing posture (as before). Now simply place your hands in your jacket pockets. If you're not wearing a jacket, or a top with pockets in, just imagine you are, placing your hands over your belly, either side of your belly button.

Now breathe deeply into your belly and feel the *chi* beginning to accumulate there. You'll feel this largely as a sensation of increasing warmth in your belly, under your hands. The heavenly globe is the *dan tien*, the seat of your energy system. And with this posture you are, indeed, warming it.

This is one of my favourite postures. I buy jumpers and tops with pockets over the belly just so that I can do it whenever I'm out and about.

The benefits of this posture

Your mind will calm down and stressful thoughts will disappear. You will strengthen the *chi* in your *dan tien* (remember, that's the engine-room of your energy system). This will help clear stagnation of blood in the body – which is particularly good for menstrual and reproductive function in women. And if – chaps – this has made you angry (you want your benefits too, of course), then remember that this exercise also stimulates liver *chi*, which will calm down any anger.

Receiving a multitude of gifts

Get into the standing posture (as before). Let your arms dangle by your sides. Then allow your palms to face forwards. Keep your arms and hands relaxed. As you breathe you'll feel the *chi* flowing into your hands. This pose opens you to the energy of the Earth and heavens. Receive whatever gifts come your way: relaxation, inspiration, healing.

The benefits of this posture

This can be the most surprising of all postures. You may feel something different every time. You may feel different sensations and experience different states of mind. It is the most open of postures, so you open to whatever you need at that time. Just be open and wait for your multitude of gifts.

The owl

Get into the standing posture (as before). Clasp your hands together behind your back: one hand holding the other and the thumbs interlocking. You'll no doubt see (contented-looking) old people standing and walking in this position. And it is, indeed, a key to a long life. I love to stand and stare at good views or bad people in this posture. And when I wander around like this I feel instantly calm.

The benefits of this posture

Your arms are cradling your kidneys, so this is very nourishing for the kidney energy system. Kidneys, remember, are the vital essence of the body – so nourishing them is a very good idea. The stretch on the arms boosts the yang meridians, so helping to warm the body.

Everything about this posture is calming and soothing.

Moving Postures

Ascending the white mountains

This posture is known in the West as cleaning your teeth. Cleaning your teeth mindfully is a truly beautiful exercise. Mainly because we so rarely think about this twice-daily activity. We just get on and do it, thinking only about what we have to do afterwards.

So it can be a beautiful exercise in mindfulness and consciousness. Treat it as you would any F**k It Form posture: make sure your knees are bent, check that you're fully relaxed, focus on the breathing. Then really feel what it's like to clean your teeth. Notice the taste of the toothpaste, how the brush feels on your gums, what your tongue is up to whilst all this is going on.

The benefits of this posture

Your dental hygiene levels will improve instantly, as you'll clean your teeth more thoroughly and carefully. Change to a toothpaste containing peppermint and you'll magnify the benefits, as this stimulates *chi* in the body. The stomach meridian is stimulated: so look after your teeth and you're looking after your stomach. If you chomp your teeth together occasionally, you'll also stimulate the vital kidney system – the first victim of stress and tiredness.

Diving in shallow lake

Known in the West as doing the washing-up. As in ascending the white mountains, diving in shallow lake is a beautiful exercise in mindfulness. Whereas cleaning your teeth is a quick, unconsidered action, doing the washing-up is a more drawn-out, and usually painful, affair. We tend to do it as fast as we can while distracting ourselves as effectively as possible (e.g. with a radio) and look forward to the whole hideous episode being over smartish. Which is why it's so good to get 'mindful' around it.

Mindfulness is all about bringing your attention to what you're doing. Rather than trying to avoid focusing on what you're doing, you deliberately keep bringing your attention back to it. You bring your attention into the present moment (when it's normally in the past or future) and into the present space and activity (when it's usually wandering around somewhere else entirely).

And I'm not the first to enter the bubbly and rubber-gloved world of washing-up as an exercise for mindfulness and meditation. The Buddhists have been chopping wood, carrying water and washing pots since pre-history.

So, use your experience from the F**k It still meditation forms to relax into a good posture, and get washing. Keep relaxing your legs and arms. Then bring your attention to what it's really like to wash pots: notice how the warm water feels (apart from warm, smart-arse), the sounds of the pots as they touch each other, the beauty of light reflecting in the washing-up bubbles.

It may be difficult to contain yourself after a couple of goes at this exercise. You'll start volunteering to do the washing-up at every possible opportunity. This will give you many points with partners, friends and relatives, but it may give you slightly rougher-looking hands, so remember to use a good moisturizer, folks.

The benefits of this posture

The mindfulness you learn in this exercise will most probably seep into the rest of your life: the shift in your perception and state of mind can be enormous and life-changing.

Simply putting your hands in warm water creates a lot of *chi* flow in the vital meridians along the arms and running into each of the fingers. These include the heart meridian (you'll feel happier), the pericardium meridian (you'll feel more open) and the lung meridian (you'll feel more free).

Wow, they should charge for letting you do the washing-up, really.

THE ENDING

Everything Ends

So here we are, the end of this book.

We could sit and talk for another few hours about whether it's true that 'everything ends': whether our soul lives on after our physical deaths, or we're reincarnated, or we reside in some 'heaven' or 'hell' for eternity, or we get to haunt those we didn't like in life.

But let's for a moment deal with the truth that either Everything Ends, or Almost Everything Ends, or At Least the Things You Care About End.

And facing that, we have to feel the sadness of it.

And facing the sadness, and feeling all our feelings, is, as you'll know by now, a rather F**k It thing to do.

We say F**k It to the tendency to skip on to the next thing, to avert our eyes from the difficult truths, to hold our breaths and not want to feel the difficulty.

So sit for a moment and feel the feelings of endings.

And as you do so, you'll probably feel two things:

The sadness of the ending.

The slowly emerging excitement of the next thing.

Feel both.

And as you close this book and move onto the next thing, carry our two-word magic-mantra with you always, my gift to you:

F**k It.

YOU'VE READ THE BOOK – NOW GO ON A F**K IT RETREAT IN ITALY

This is where it all started: John and Gaia ran their first F**k It Retreat in 2005. They're now running these famous retreats in spectacular locations around Italy, including an estate and spa in Urbino, and on the volcano of Stromboli. Say F**k It and treat yourself to a F**k It Retreat.

'Anything that helps you let go is okay on a F**k It Retreat.' THE OBSERVER
'I witnessed some remarkable transformations during my F**k It Retreat.' KINDRED SPIRIT

F**KIT
RETREATS

LIVE THE F**K IT LIFE   WWW.THEFUCKITLIFE.COM

YOU'VE READ THE BOOK — NOW TRY A F**K IT ONLINE COURSE
and explore John & Gaia's teaching from anywhere in the world.

ABOUT THE AUTHOR

The son of Anglican preachers, **John C. Parkin** realized that saying F**k It was as powerful as all the Eastern spiritual practices he'd been studying for 20 years.

Having said F**k It to their jobs and lives in London, he and his partner, Gaia, escaped to Italy in 2004, baby twin boys in tow, to establish a retreat centre and live the life. They had the epiphany of realizing that F**k It was a spiritual way and were soon teaching 'F**k It Retreats' and writing F**k It books (starting with the original *F**k It: The Ultimate Spiritual Way*).

They are now back in the UK, living near the beach in Brighton-Hove, continuing to spread the liberating message of F**k It with the world via retreats and online magic, such as the membership programme 'F**k It Revolution'.

www.thefuckitlife.com

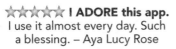

Hay House Podcasts
Bring Fresh, Free Inspiration Each Week!

Hay House proudly offers a selection of life-changing audio content via our most popular podcasts!

Hay House Meditations Podcast

Features your favorite Hay House authors guiding you through meditations designed to help you relax and rejuvenate. Take their words into your soul and cruise through the week!

Dr. Wayne W. Dyer Podcast

Discover the timeless wisdom of Dr. Wayne W. Dyer, world-renowned spiritual teacher and affectionately known as "the father of motivation." Each week brings some of the best selections from the 10-year span of Dr. Dyer's talk show on Hay House Radio.

Hay House Podcast

Enjoy a selection of insightful and inspiring lectures from Hay House Live events, listen to some of the best moments from previous Hay House Radio episodes, and tune in for exclusive interviews and behind-the-scenes audio segments featuring leading experts in the fields of alternative health, self-development, intuitive medicine, success, and more! Get motivated to live your best life possible by subscribing to the free Hay House Podcast.

Find Hay House podcasts on iTunes, or visit www.HayHouse.com/podcasts for more info.

CONNECT WITH
HAY HOUSE
ONLINE

🌐 hayhouse.co.uk   **f** @hayhouse

📷 @hayhouseuk   🐦 @hayhouseuk

▶️ @hayhouseuk   🎵 @hayhouseuk

Find out all about our latest books & card decks • Be the first to know about exclusive discounts • Interact with our authors in live broadcasts • Celebrate the cycle of the seasons with us • Watch free videos from your favourite authors • Connect with like-minded souls

'The gateways to wisdom and knowledge are always open.'

Louise Hay